HILTON WUHAN OPTICS VALLEY

The Story of a Landmark Resort

images
Publishing

Published in Australia in 2017 by
The Images Publishing Group Pty Ltd
Shanghai Office
ABN 89 059 734 431
6 Bastow Place, Mulgrave, Victoria 3170, Australia
Tel: +61 3 9561 5544 Fax: +61 3 9561 4860
books@imagespublishing.com
www.imagespublishing.com

Title: Hilton Wuhan Optics Valley
Author: XU Qi (ed.)
ISBN: 9781864707229

For Catalogue-in-Publication data, please see the National Library of Australia entry

Printed by Everbest Printing Investment Limited., Hong Kong/China

IMAGES has included on its website a page for special notices in relation to this and our other
publications. Please visit www.imagespublishing.com

Contents

Introduction

Introduction

Hilton Wuhan Optics Valley ("the Hotel" or "the Project"), located along the Yanxi Lake in Wuhan Huashan Ecological New Town ("Huashan New Town" or "the Town"), is a joint development by Hubei United Investment Group and Country Garden Group. Built to the standard specifications of Hilton's flagship resort, Hilton Wuhan Optics Valley is the biggest, the most multi-functional, state-of-the-art hotel for state guests. It is the business and convention center for the Donghu High-tech Zone, as well as a prime hub for political and business activities.

The Hotel is about a 30-minute drive from downtown Wuhan, and a 50-minute drive from Wuhan Tianhe International Airport; it is close to Wuhan Train Station, Happy Valley, and the city's new expressway. It is in a prime location yet close to nature, making the Hotel a top choice for business and leisure guests.

Taking up 20 hectares of site area and 110,000 square meters of gross floor area, the Project incorporates a hotel, a convention center, a spa, and an entertainment center, covering the four functions of resort-style accommodation: meetings and receptions, banquets, leisure, and entertainment. The hotel component comprises 515 luxury guest rooms and suites—all with private balconies overlooking the beautiful Yanxi Lake. The Hotel also boasts a 5000-square-meter convention center with a 1818-square-meter zero-pillar banquet hall and an outdoor ceremonial lawn—an ideal location for social galas and business meetings. In addition, the Hotel is equipped with various entertainment and leisure facilities, including a 1600-square-meter spa area, a 3600-square-meter entertainment center, an indoor heated swimming pool, an outdoor swimming pool, a gym, a cycling route, a lakeside basketball court, and a tennis court.

The renowned architect Ling Kege and his team led the overall design of the Hilton Wuhan Optics Valley; Hirsch Bedner Associates (HBA) took charge of the interior design while Peridian International oversaw the landscape architecture and planning. It took three years of hard work and collaboration by these leading international and national designers before the team was able to present to Wuhan this product of fine design. The overall design of the Hotel was well thought out:

tightly knit around the core area yet spaced out at the outset, the layout features a symmetry and a separation of the external and the internal areas. The creative use of a cluster of courtyards interlacing with each other characterizes the hotel lobby. The functional areas are thus separated so that the guests can enjoy an experience of unique spaces typically offered only by small hotels. The design of the façade drew inspiration from Jing-chu culture—clean lines, delicate details, traditional textures, and natural materials—and imparted a sense of understated luxury and otherworldly elegance, allowing the architecture of the Hotel to perfectly blend into the natural environment around the Yanxi Lake.

The design of the Hotel, awarded the National Green Architecture Model Project Medal, reflects the world's leading ecological principles, systematically uses multiple energy-saving measures, and achieves a symbiotic harmony between the

architecture and the environment. A ground-source thermal pump was analyzed and endorsed by an authoritative panel of experts led by Wang Jiyang, of the China Academy of Science, as a new technology for energy saving. The Hotel's centralized ground-source thermal pump, the biggest of its kind in Central China, takes advantage of the moderate temperature of the ground to reduce the energy consumption of the air-conditioning systems by 20—40%.

The completion of Hilton Wuhan Optics Valley is owed to the collective effort by the owners, the designers, and the constructors; it is a critical milestone in Central China's development. This book showcases various stages of the Project—from early-stage preparation to design and engineering, and finally to construction and completion—as well as the hard work of the entire team behind the Project.

Site

"Pearls in central China"

Site

• Huashan New Town: An ecological model for the development of Central China

Wuhan, situated in the east of Jianghan Plain of China, is well known for its history and culture. A central city in Central China and a national hub of industry, science and education, as well as transportation, Wuhan has established its prominence in the development of Central China.

Huashan New Town, in the north of the city's Donghu High-tech Zone, sits where "One River and Three Lakes" (namely, the Yangtze River, the Bei Lake, the Yanxi Lake, and the Yandong Lake) join together. The Town, with a total area of 66.4 square kilometers and a population of close to 200,000, takes a central position in east Wuhan's urban development zone. The development of Huashan New Town focuses on the areas of ecological R&D and trade, ecological hotel and convention, ecological commerce and entertainment, and ecological living and leisure, to create an ecological new town for living, leisure, R&D, and commerce. Developed under the guidelines of Wuhan's "two-oriented society" (resources-conserving and environmentally-friendly) strategy, Huashan New Town is set to be a model for urban development, a strategic milestone in China's ecological development, a first of its kind in Central China and an internationally renowned ecological town.

| Bird's-eye view of Huashan New Town

The Central City of Wuhan

Yangtze River

Dong Lake

Huashan New Town

Tangxun Lake

Donghu High-tech Zone

| The location of Huashan New Town in Wuhan City

The pristine landscape of wetlands in Huashan
New Town

- **Huashan New Town's "bridgehead": resources of a pristine wetland**

The development of Wuhan Hilton Optics Valley marked the official launch of Huashan New Town. Spanning 20 hectares, the Hotel is in the west of the Town and sits to the west of Huashan Avenue, to the north of Wujiu Railway, to the east of Yanxi Lake, and to the south of Huacheng Avenue. Such a prime location makes the Hotel a "bridgehead"—a strategic landmark—of the Town.

The Hotel's site also enjoys unparalleled proximity to natural beauty: with mountains at the back and waters in the front, the scenery is exquisite and the environment splendid. The Gujia Mountain sits across the lake in the northwest of the Project, the Changjia Mountain in the northeast, the Jiufeng Mountain Forrest Park in the southeast, and the Yanxi Lake, wide and open, in the south—all are invaluable natural resources.

The landform of the site features ridges, clay and hilly, with multiple ponds scattered around and endowed with a rare pristine wetland. The local vegetation mainly includes local plants and common agricultural products, such as lotus flowers, bok choy, platycarya, azaleas, rhododendron simsii, ligustrum lucidum, glochidion, and camphor trees.

Downtown
Wuhan

650m
420m

Yanxi Lake

Project location—Huashan New Town's
bridgehead

| The great bridge stretching across Yanxi Lake

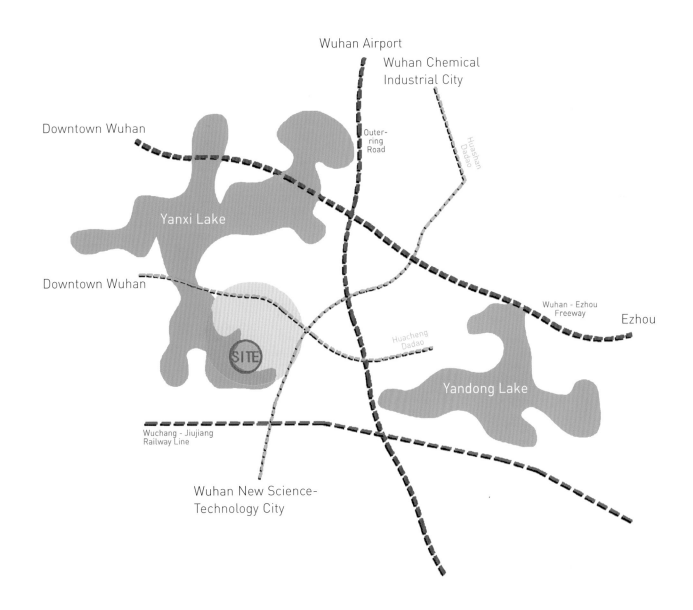

Wuhan Airport

Wuhan Chemical
Industrial City

Downtown Wuhan

Outer-
ring
Road

Huashan
Dadao

Yanxi Lake

Downtown Wuhan

Wuhan - Ezhou
Freeway

Ezhou

Huacheng
Dadao

Yandong Lake

Wuchang - Jiujiang
Railway Line

Wuhan New Science-
Technology City

| Traffic conditions of the project site

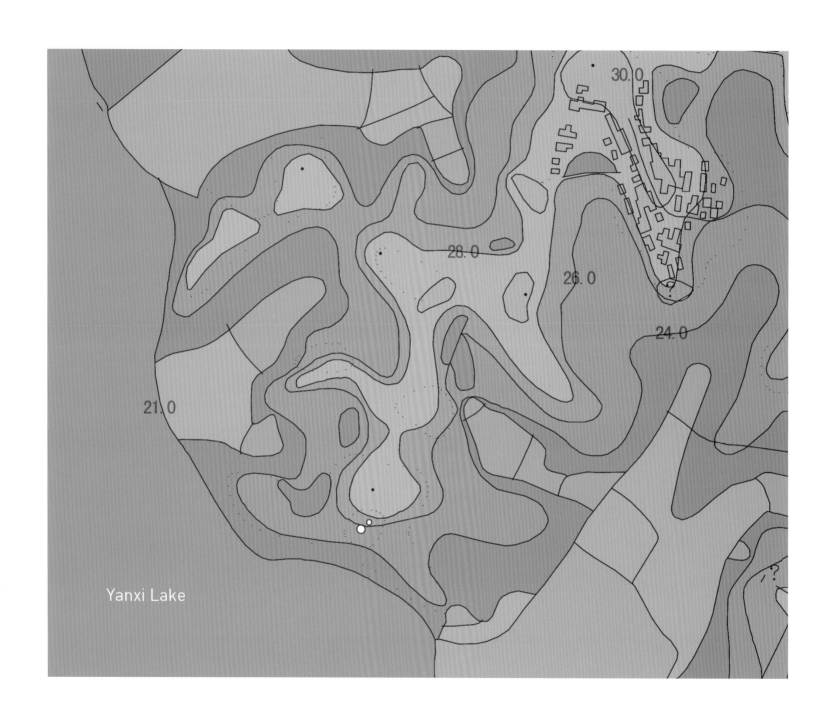

30.0

28.0

26.0

24.0

21.0

Yanxi Lake

| Landform and typology: gentle slope and wetland

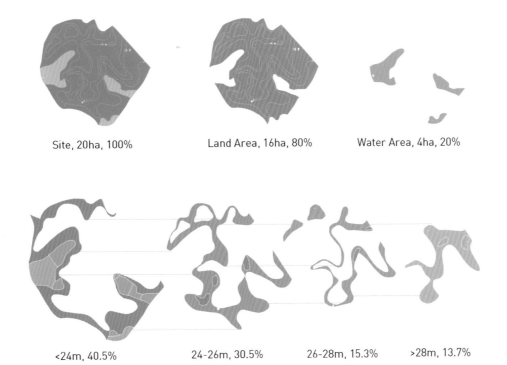

Site, 20ha, 100%   Land Area, 16ha, 80%   Water Area, 4ha, 20%

<24m, 40.5%   24-26m, 30.5%   26-28m, 15.3%   >28m, 13.7%

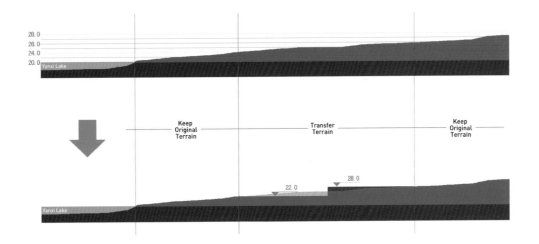

Top | Land and water area ratio
Middle | Typical altitude—area ratio
Bottom | Sections of the project site

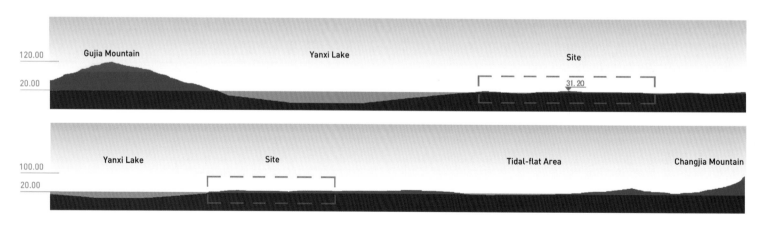

120.00
20.00

Gujia Mountain   Yanxi Lake   Site
31.20

100.00
20.00

Yanxi Lake   Site   Tidal-flat Area   Changjia Mountain

Top | Wetland landscape resources
Bottom | Sections of the wetland

| Rich wetland plants

Landscape resources

The base has diverse landscape resources due to its rich topography. The Yanxi Lake provides it with a shoreline that equals half of its perimeter, giving the base a broad view. The Gujia Mountain across the lake, the Jiufeng Mountain Forest Park on the south as well as the wetland park to be built form a beautiful surrounding. These wonderful natural environment conditions makes the base a a perfect place for resort development.

| View analysis

| Mountains, lakes, and wetlands

Concept

"A pastoral symphony of paradise"

Concept

Resort guests typically travel far for a unique experience beyond what a functional and comfortable hotel provides. The theme and the concept of the design, as well as the subsequent execution, determines if the resort can ignite in the guests a sense of longing for nature and for life. The Hotel's designers thoroughly considered all key factors and adhered to the following three principles for the design of the Hotel:

- **To use passive ecological technology to build an environmentally friendly hotel**

In line with internationally recognized ecological principles, the design of the Hotel incorporates passive ecological energy-saving technologies and measures, including natural ecological measures, energy-saving measures for construction, the use of recyclable energies, and intelligent control and energy management systems, in order to build an environmentally friendly hotel and achieve a harmonious symbiotic relationship between the architecture and the nature.

- **To bring an experience of unique spaces**

Hilton Wuhan Optics Valley is is a very large hotel so, it is difficult to completely break away from the traditional model of large-scale centralized hotels. Nevertheless, the design team still managed to be creative in bringing out a sense of intimacy in the spatial design—a feature often unique to small boutique hotels—so that even at such a large centralized hotel, the guests can have a different kind of resort experience. The landscape undulates, at places subdued and at places audacious, and the scenery changes every step of the way. The experience of unique spaces is at the heart of the Hotel's design.

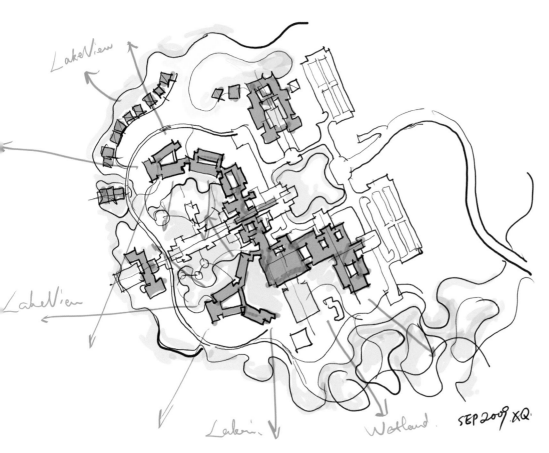

Lake View

Lake View

Lake View

Wetland.

SEP 2009 XQ.

• **To best leverage the natural resources**

The Hotel's site is endowed with treasured landscape resources—mountains at the back and waters in the front, and luxuriant plants and wetlands abound. The design team aimed to best leverage the natural landscape resources, and focused on the variety, the recreational functions, and the preservation of the natural scenery. The team further introduced elements of oriental culture to create a beautiful, otherworldly environment.

The hotel is designed to best leverage the natural resources.

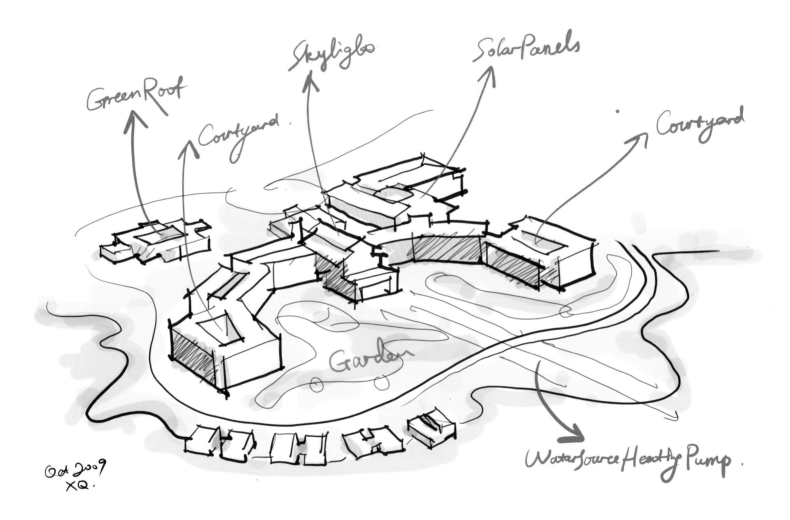

GreenRoof

Courtyard

Skylights

SolarPanels

Courtyard

Garden

Oct 2009
XQ.

WaterSource HeatPump.

Passive ecological techniques are used to build
an environmentally friendly hotel.

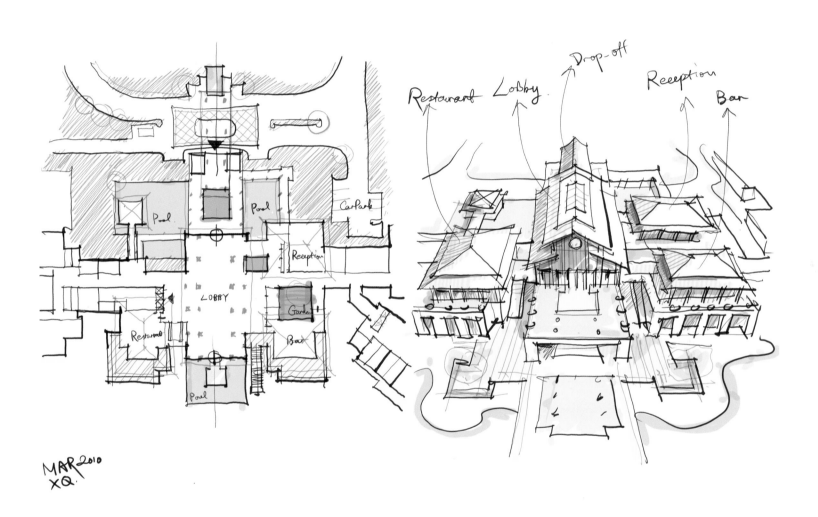

Restaurant Lobby Drop-off Reception Bar

Pool

Pool

Car Park

Reception

LOBBY

Garden

Restaurant

Bar

Pool

MAR 2010
XQ.

| The hotel brings an experience of unique spaces.

Design

"Scale is fleeting, beauty is forever"

Design

- **Overall design**

Hilton Wuhan Optics Valley is an ultra-large resort hotel of over 110,000 square meters and over 500 guest rooms—these parameters exceed those of an ordinary resort hotel. Such a large scale puts the service lines and the lobby-to-room distance to the test. From a functional perspective, it is difficult to completely break away from the traditional model of large-scale centralized hotels, given the shape of the site is similar to that of an airport terminal plus concourses.

Through appropriate analysis, the design team eventually used the classical layout of "one main body and two wings": the public lounge in the lobby serves as the main body, and the guest rooms are spread out across the eastern and the western wings. The lobby also separates the external area (including the convention center, the spa, and the entertainment center), which operates independently and is open to the public, from the internal area of guest rooms where privacy is important. Such a division allows the two areas, one relatively action-packed, and the other relatively quiet, to properly perform their functions.

The layout was further aimed at best leveraging the landscape resources—the Hotel stretches along the meandering banks of the lake to maximize the exposure to the waterscape and to allow most guest rooms lake views. At the same time, two gardens—one in the lobby and the other outside—add to the variety of scenery and allow the guests to enjoy different sights as they walk around.

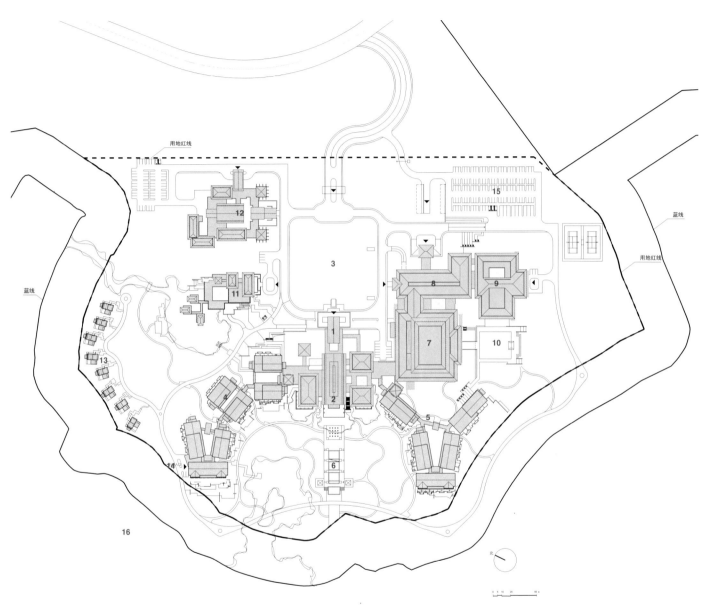

用地红线

蓝线

蓝线

用地红线

16

1	Drop-off	7	Ballrooms	13	Villas
2	Lobby	8	Meeting rooms	14	Executive lobby
3	Entrance	9	International convention center	15	Parking
4	West-wing guest rooms	10	Wedding lawn	16	Yanxi lake
5	East-wing guest rooms	11	Spa		
6	Central garden	12	Recreational		

| Master plan

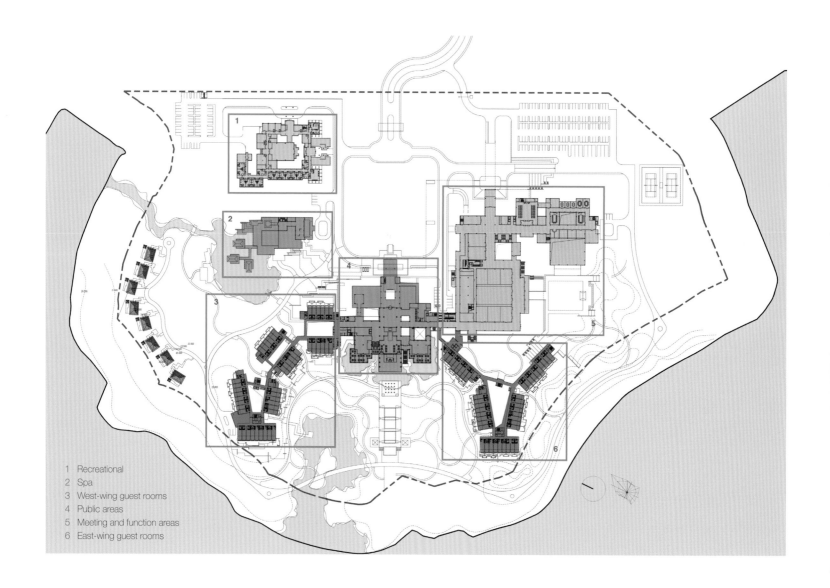

1 Recreational
2 Spa
3 West-wing guest rooms
4 Public areas
5 Meeting and function areas
6 East-wing guest rooms

A classical model of large-scale centralized hotels:
one main body with two wings and a clear separation of
the outer-inter functional zone

| Functional area plan

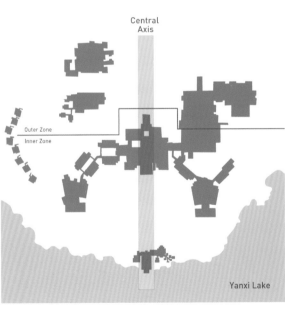

Central
Axis

Outer Zone
Inner Zone

Yanxi Lake

The hotel features a central symmetry and a clear
separation of the outer and inner zones.

Hotel

Central Garden

Lake

A layout stretching along the lake maximizes the
lake view

Top | View analysis
Opposite | Master plan of the overall landscape design

Pavilion   Public areas   Front canopy

Western restaurant   All-day dining   Bar   Reception desk and administrative offices

- **The design of the lobby**

The design of the lobby reflects the essence of the Hotel's overall design concept. Different from other hotels' centralized lobbies, the lobby of Hilton Wuhan Optics Valley consists of a few spaces connected through a cluster of courtyards interlacing each other. The public lounge is in the center of the lobby, while the check-in hall, the Western restaurant and the bar flank the lounge, just like what the Chinese call "the stars surround the moon". Connected by the criss-crossing corridors and the varied courtyards, the functional areas stand as individual spaces. The whole lobby area is creatively divided into smaller parts to give the guests an experience of unique spaces. This is a major innovation in the design of a large centralized resort hotel. During the design process, the team conducted much research on the hotel service lines and the guest flows to eventually come up the design for the lobby.

Once alighted at the Hotel's front canopy, guests enter a tranquil courtyard. Through the long corridors, they reach the public lounge and appreciate the beautiful scenery along the way—the water flows, the trees abound, the birds chirp, and the flowers emanate pleasant fragrances. Guests are blown away by the spectacular lake-and-mountain view from the lounge and the large space of the central lounge. From the lounge and through a corridor, guests arrive at the check-in hall, which stands on its own. Taking into account the large number of convention guests and group travelers, the design team uses the courtyard layout to separate different types of guests. The central lounge, instead of being used as a front desk, now serves to build a unique image of the Hotel and to function as an observation deck. With this creative arrangement, the Hotel's lobby is not even crowded during the peak seasons. The use of courtyards to connect various spaces is ubiquitous throughout the Hotel, letting in sunshine, introducing greenery, bringing in natural light, and allowing ventilation. The lobby, with the skylight as an additional lighting feature, is bright enough without any artificial lighting during the daytime—one of the key features that won the Project the Two Star Green Award.

The introduction of the skylight is the most attractive feature of the lobby, but it was challenging to construct the sprung roof. The roof structure is entirely in the open and yet the wiring must be hidden. A tremendous amount of hard work went into eventually resolving such a puzzle. During the process, the design team had multiple rounds of building and rebuilding the models and communicating with the structural engineers for fine-tuning, before completing the setup of over 400 beams. Further, the designers covered up the ventilation windows in the cloisters on the two sides of the lobby by tucking these windows under the beams and camouflaging them with window grills, making them invisible to most guests. The result is a neat and bright lobby, one of the best in ambience and finishing among all resort hotels in China with similar weather conditions.

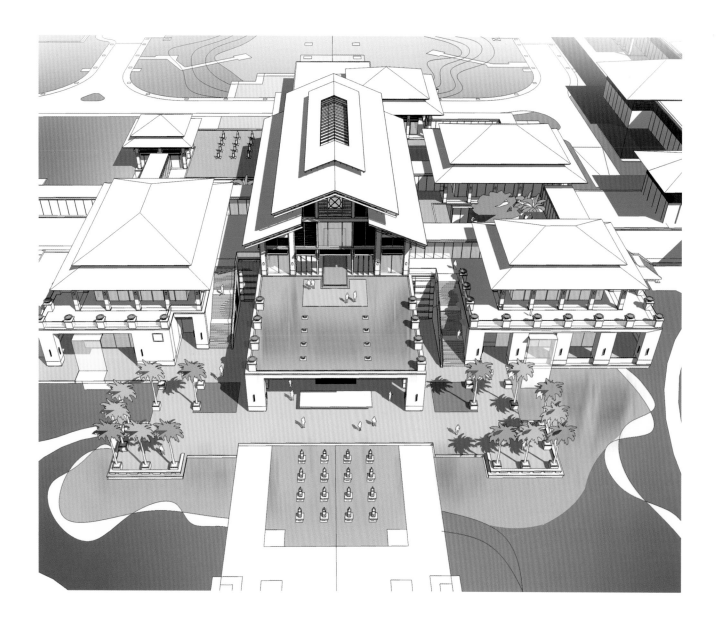

A creative layout of courtyards in clusters: the
whole lobby area is divided into smaller parts to
give the guests an experience of unique spaces.

I Design model of the lobby

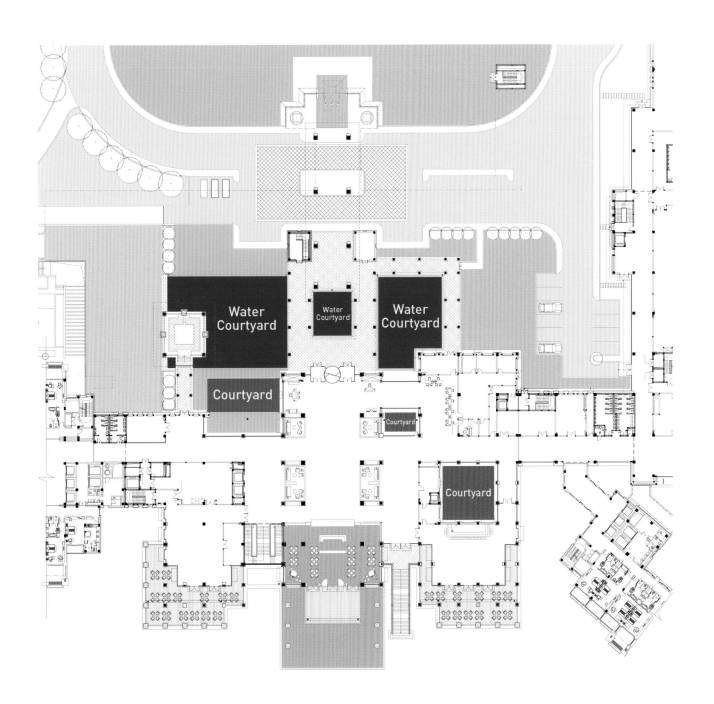

Water Courtyard

Water Courtyard

Water Courtyard

Courtyard

Courtyard

Courtyard

| Courtyard analysis scheme of the lobby

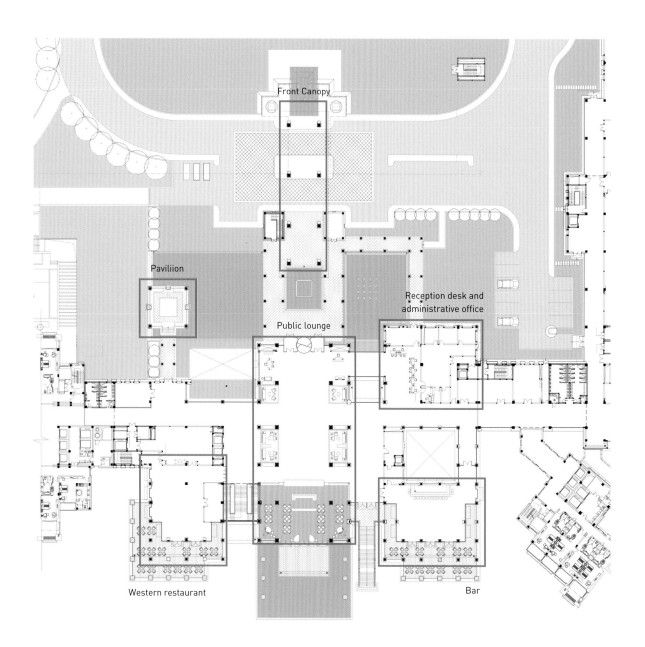

Front Canopy

Paviliion

Reception desk and
administrative office

Public lounge

Western restaurant

Bar

A creative layout of courtyards in clusters: the
whole lobby area is divided into smaller parts to
give the guests an experience of unique spaces.

| Functional analysis scheme of the lobby

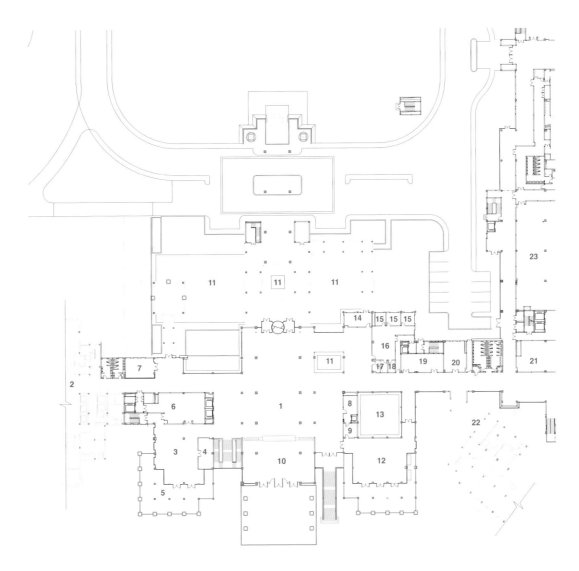

1   Lobby

2   Guest rooms

3   Italian restaurant, Cucina

4   Private dining rooms

5   Outdoor parking

6   Kitchen of Italian restaurant

7   Gift shop

8   Lobby lounge service

9   Bar service

10 Lobby lounge

11 Water feature

12 Bar, El Valle

13 Open to below

14 Luggage room

15 Office

16 Reception

17 Safe deposit

18 Pantry

19 Business center

20 Reservation office

21 F&B stores

22 Guest rooms

23 Kitchen of ballrooms

| Plan of the lobby

▼ Waterfront terrace   ▼ Outdoor swimming pool   ▼ Central garden   ▼ Public areas

The lobby provides a great view of Yanxi Lake.

Entrance sequence from entry garden, drop-off canopy,
courtyard, lobby, central garden to waterfront terrace

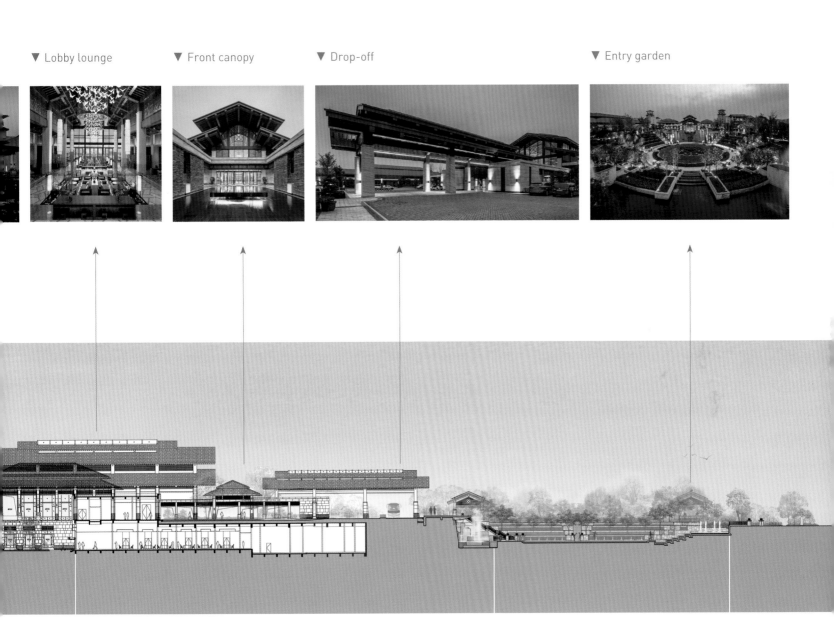

▼ Lobby lounge ▼ Front canopy ▼ Drop-off ▼ Entry garden

Lake

Reflective
water

Lamp

Corridor dining

Full-time restaurant

Lobby

Kitchen

Penetrable lobby provide a great view of Yanxi Lake.

I Sections of the lobby

Skylight

Corridor

Service administration

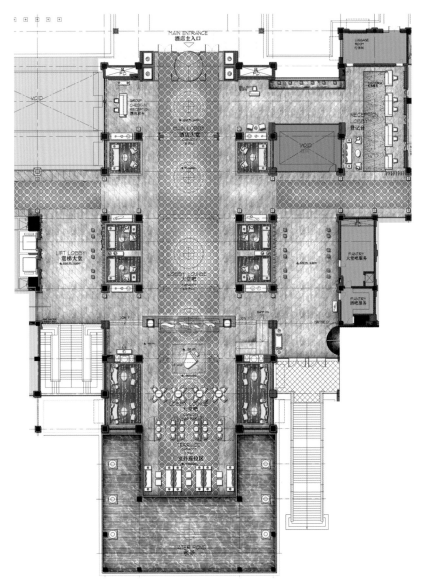

| Plan of the lobby lounge

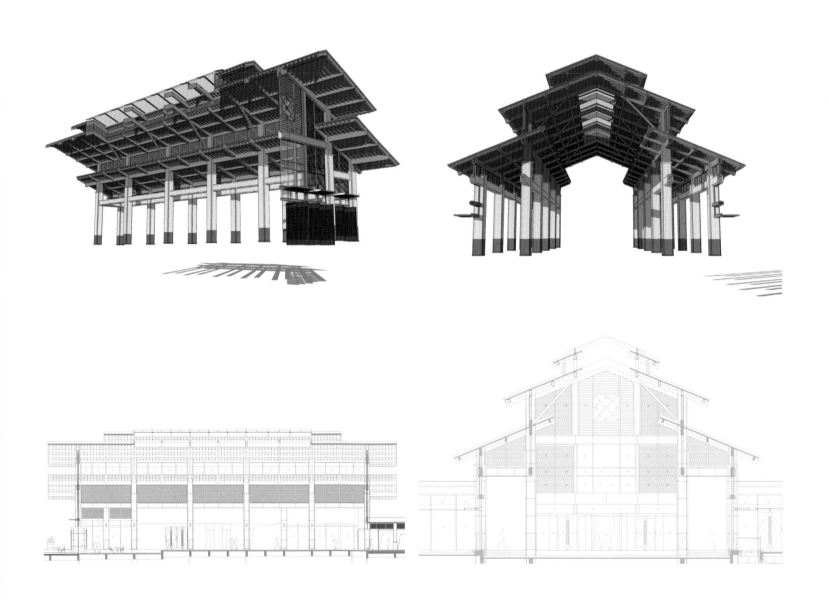

Primitive lobby design introduces natural light.

Top and bottom | Primitive wooden roof takes place of sprung roof.
Opposite | Natural light is introduced through the skylight.

| The magnificent resort-style lobby

• **The design of the meeting and function area**

The Hotel has an ultra-large meeting and function area. The banquet area features two halls. One of them has a floor area of 1818-square-meters without any pillar. It is connected to an outdoor ceremonial lawn, and the two spaces altogether can accommodate 3500 dining guests. The international convention center has close to 20 conference rooms of various sizes and the biggest multi-function conference room can seat 2000 guests.

Wedding lawn

The international
convention center

Guest rooms

Grand ballrooms

Wedding pavilion

Barbecue area

Waterfront promenade

The banquet and convention area is L-shaped, revealing the view at the ceremonial lawn. The lawn was constructed to suit the local topography and is connected to the reception area of the large banquet hall by way of a ceremonial bridge. The flow from the outdoor wedding ceremony to the indoor wedding banquet is perfectly smooth. The indoor swimming pool on the first floor overlooks the wall cascade on one side of the lawn, and the two spaces are connected seamlessly.

Yanxi Lake

Guest rooms

Ballrooms

The international convention center

Wedding pavilion

Wedding lawn

Gentle slope with groves

Gentle slope with a lake view

| Wedding lawn

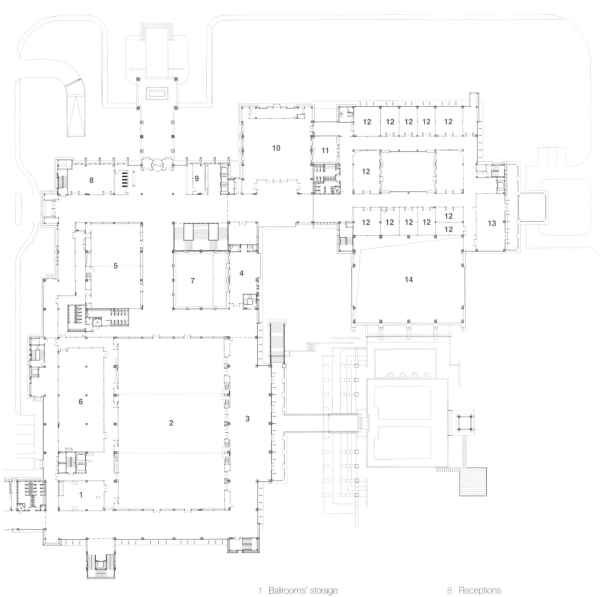

1 Ballrooms' storage
2 Grand ballrooms
3 Pre-function areas of the ballrooms
4 VIP room
5 Small ballrooms
6 Kitchen of ballrooms
7 Internal courtyard

8 Receptions
9 Front desk
10 Presence chamber
11 Internal courtyard
12 Meeting rooms
13 Boardrooms
14 The international conventional center

| Plan of the meeting and function area

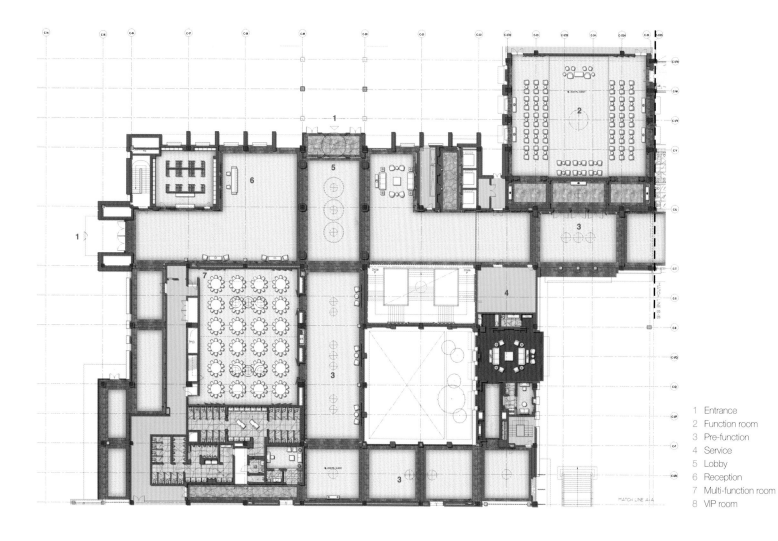

1 Entrance
2 Function room
3 Pre-function
4 Service
5 Lobby
6 Reception
7 Multi-function room
8 VIP room

Small ballrooms and the entrance of meeting
rooms

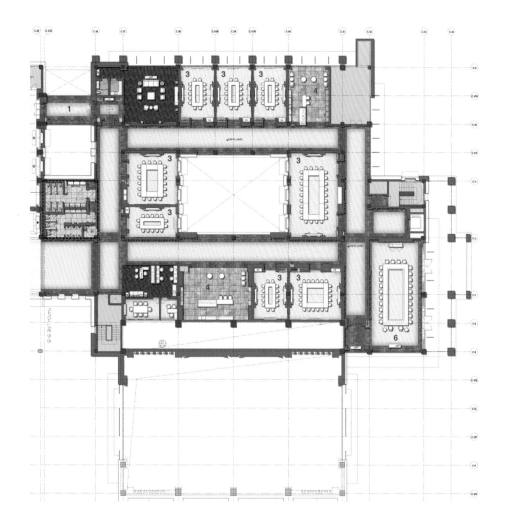

1 Function meeting foyer
2 VIP room
3 Meeting room
4 Break-out area
5 Business center
6 Boardroom

| Plan of the meeting rooms

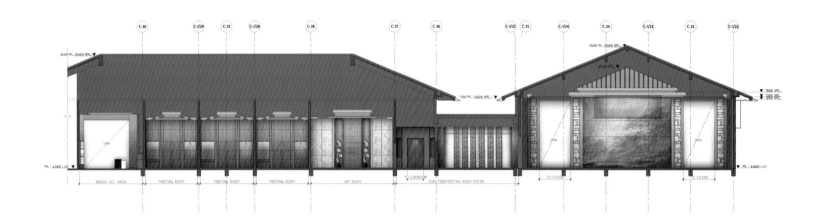

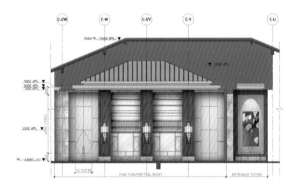
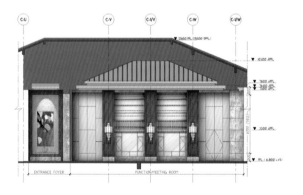

Elevations of the function room, VIP room,
meeting rooms and break-out area

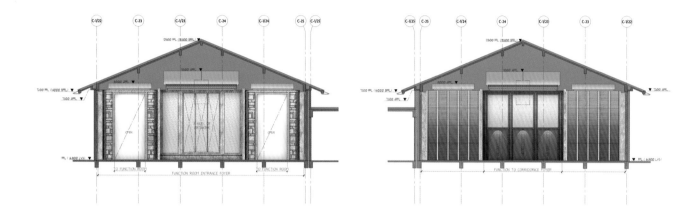

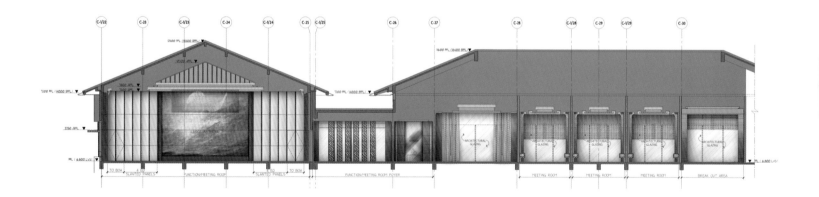

| Elevation of the function room

69   Hilton Wuhan Optics Valley

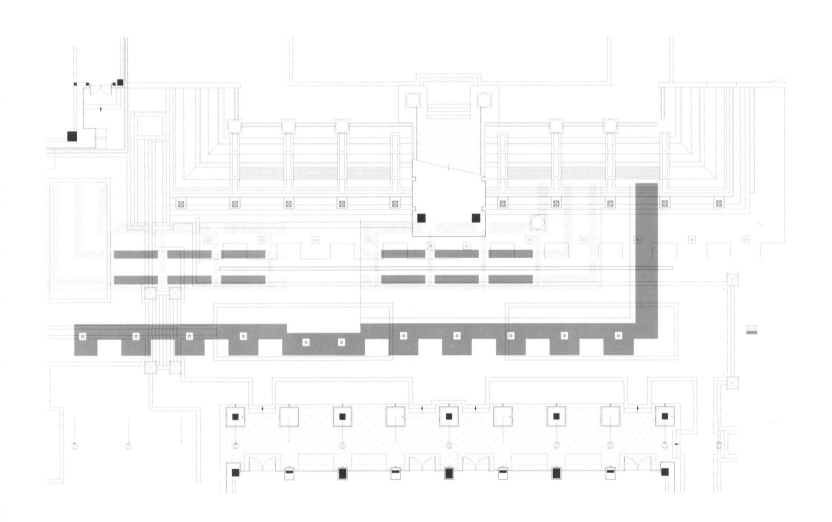

Sunken cascade garden and the Magpie Bridge

| Plan

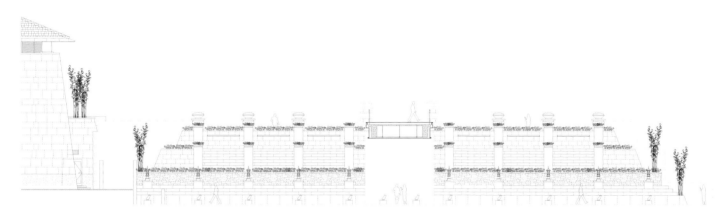

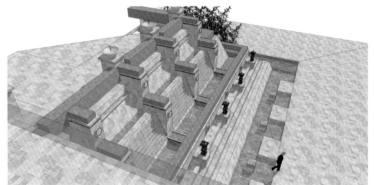

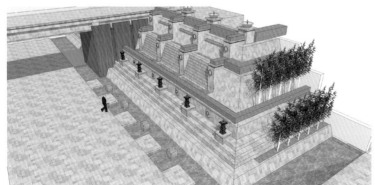

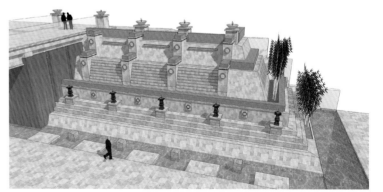

| Elevation and renderings

Sunken cascade garden and the Magpie Bridge

| A realized image of the sunken cascade garden
and Magpie Bridge

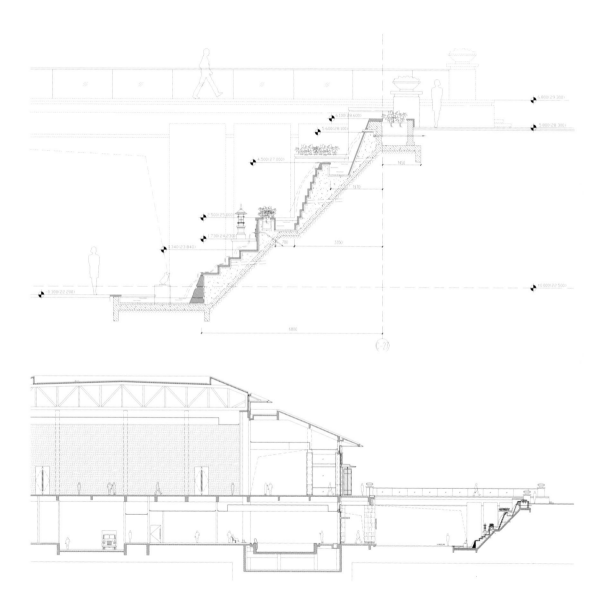

Wedding lawn

| A realized image of the wedding lawn

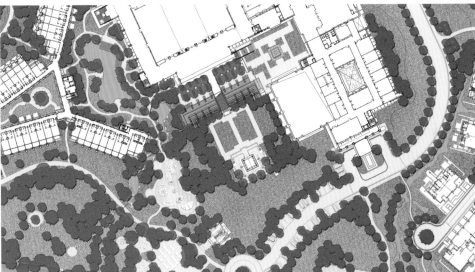

Top | Master plan
Bottom | The wedding pavilion

75   Hilton Wuhan Optics Valley

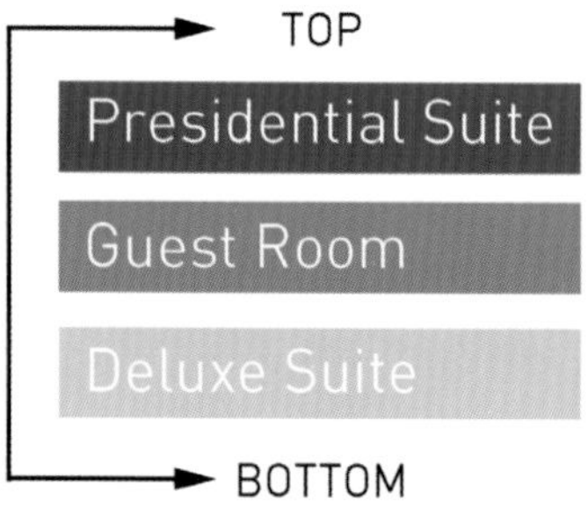

TOP

Presidential Suite

Guest Room

Deluxe Suite

BOTTOM

- **The design of the guest room area**

The 515 guest rooms and suites in the east and the west wings spread out along the lake to maximize the exposure to the waterscape and to allow most guest rooms to have lake views. Such a large number of guest rooms implies a maximum lobby-to-room distance of over 200 meters if the rooms are laid out in a straight line as is usually the case, while a reasonable maximum distance should be 160 meters. In order to solve this problem, the designers came to a two-tier solution. First, the executive rooms are kept at the far end, where the view is the best, and an independent executive lobby was set up on the first floor to allow executive room guests separate access. The standard rooms are laid out on both sides of the interior corridor so that the distance from the core area of the Hotel to the furthest standard room is reduced to 170 meters. Second, in order to make the walk to the room more delightful, various courtyards are joined to the internal corridor. As a guest walks along the corridor to their room, they can enjoy various views and spaces; the arrival experience is enhanced. The room service team works at the basement of the Hotel, and reaches the service centers of different levels through the service lifts in different zones. The maximum distance from a service center to a room is capped at 25 meters to ensure the quality of service.

| Sections of guest rooms

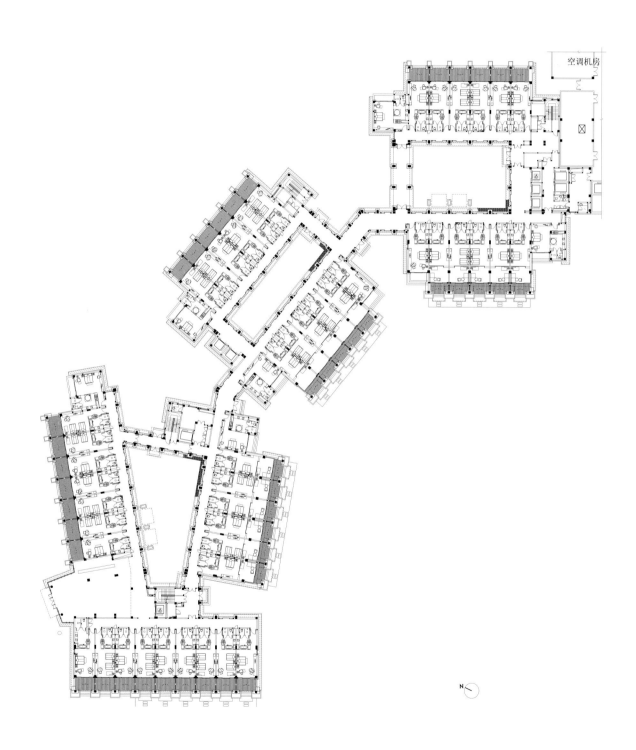

空调机房

I Ground floor plan of west-wing guest rooms

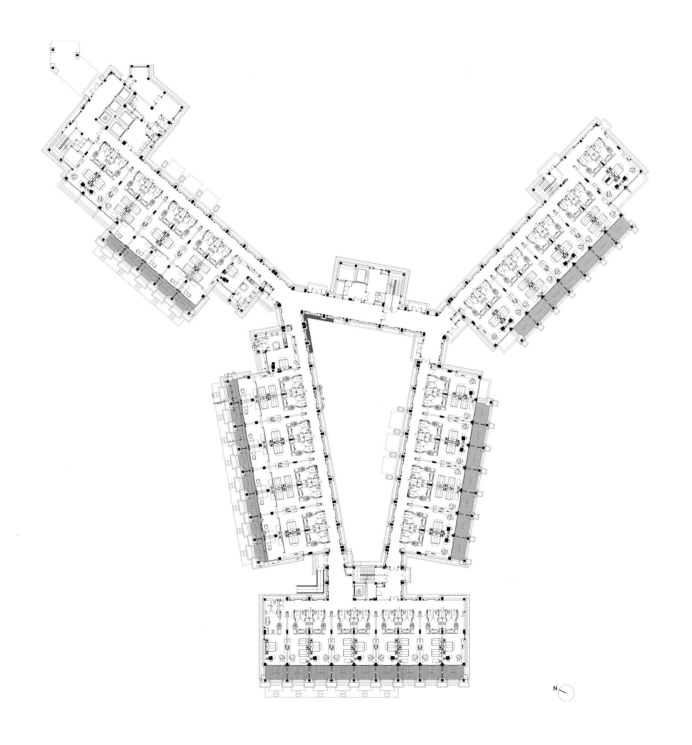

I Ground floor plan of east-wing guest rooms

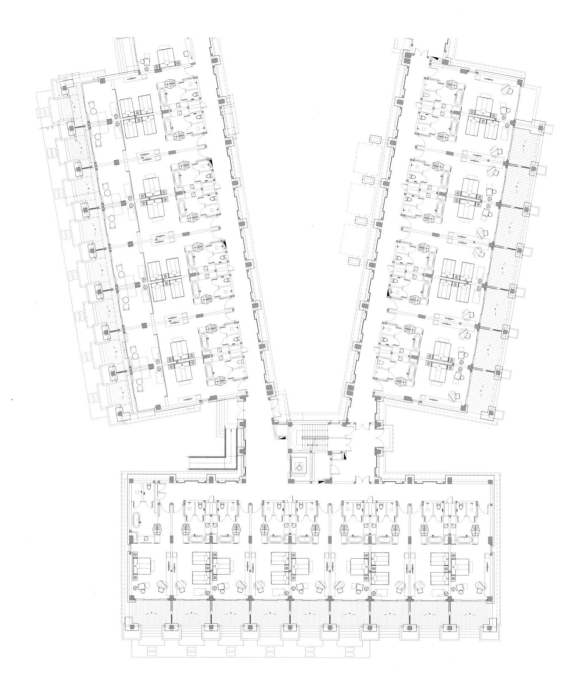

One side of the corridors to guest rooms is
connected with internal courtyards, providing
natural light and delightful landscape.

I Plan of guest rooms and internal courtyard

| A realized image of the corridors to guest rooms

Design details highlight the resort style of the Hotel.

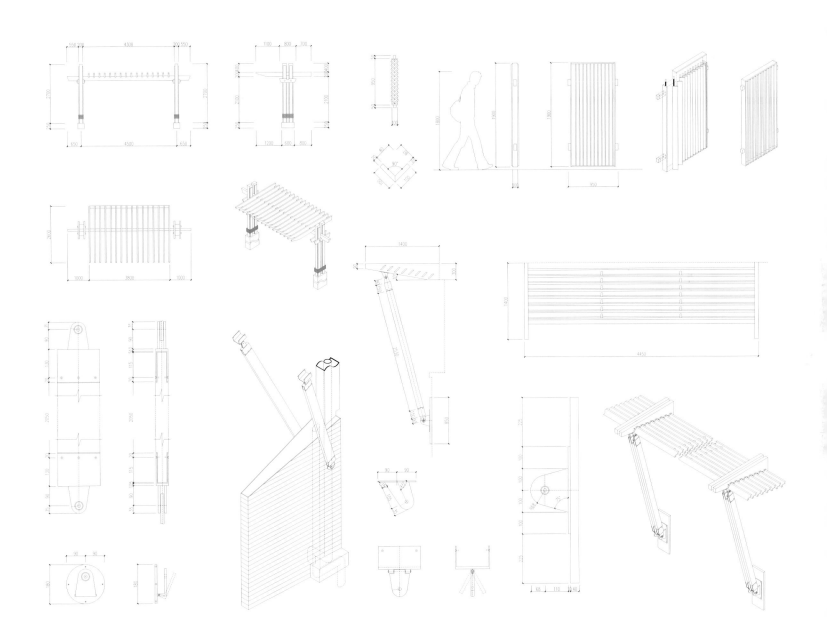

| Drawings of the details

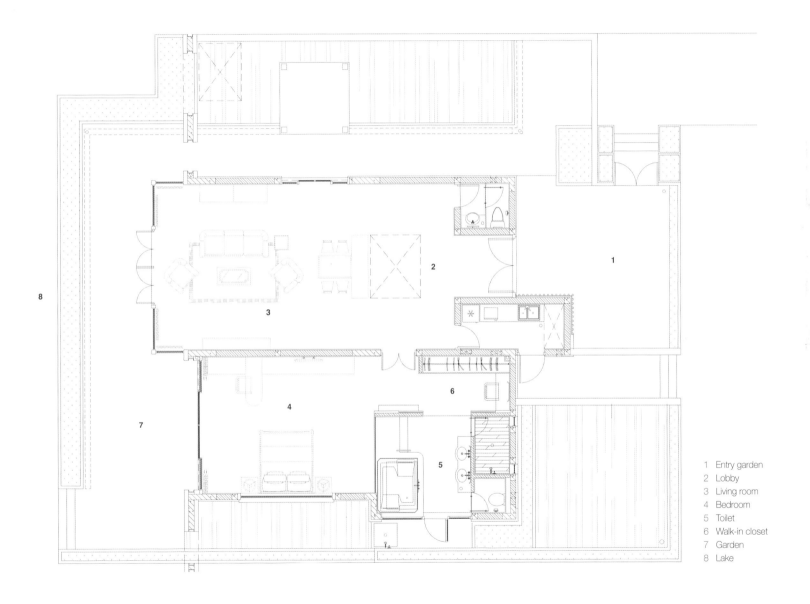

1 Entry garden
2 Lobby
3 Living room
4 Bedroom
5 Toilet
6 Walk-in closet
7 Garden
8 Lake

| Plan of villas

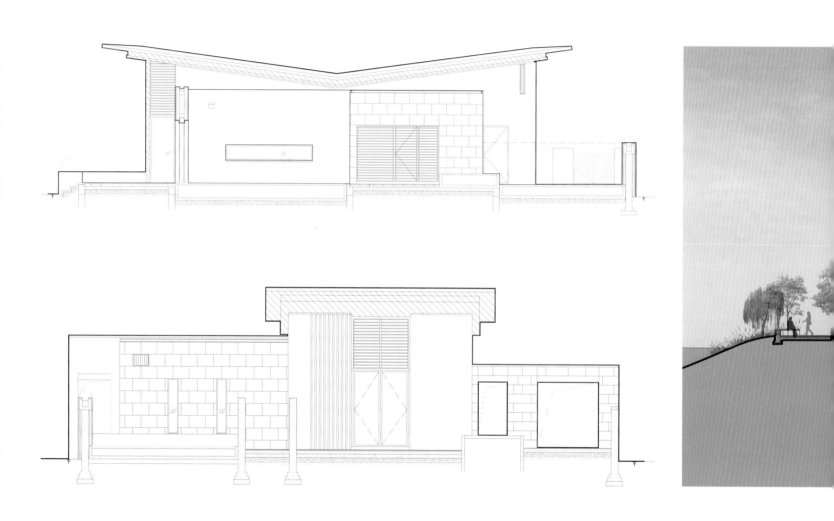

| Elevations of villas

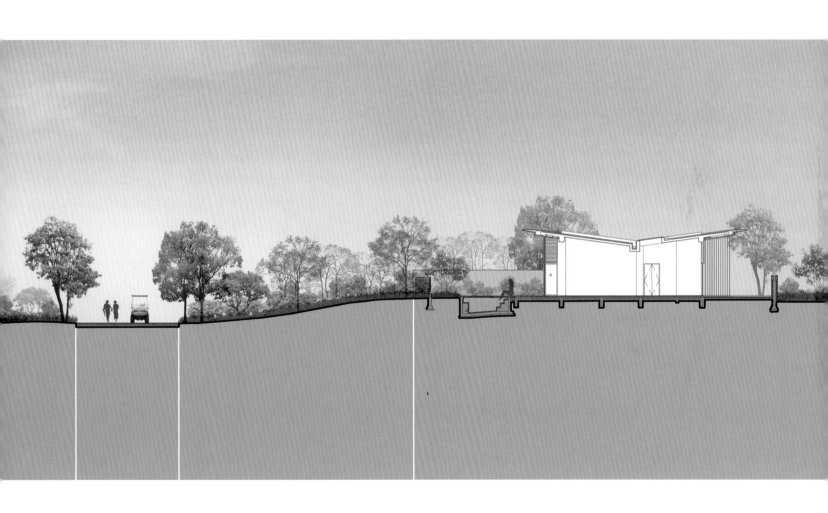

Elevation design strikes balance between a
sense of ceremony and that of a resort.

3.2   2.5   4.7   5   1.4

4.10

4.4

2.1   2.6   2.7   2.6

1.4
Coating

2.1
Cream dry-hang sandstone

2.5
Off-white dry-hang travertine

2.6
Auburn rough dry-hang stone

2.7
Black galaxy dry-hang granite

2.8
Stacked-slate wall surface

3.2
Carbonized anti-corrosive teakwood wall panel

3.3
Carbonized anti-corrosive teakwood plate

4.7
Gray fluorocarbon coating aluminum alloy eaves

5
Dark gray pottery flat tile

☐
Vertically exposed and horizontally hidden frame glass wall

☐
Wood-like aluminum alloy awning

☐
Light

☐
Candlestick

• The design of the façade

The design of the façade is based on the traditional structures of a Chinese hip roof and the fundamental features of an open lakeside resort hotel. The structural lines are clean, the details are delicate; the appropriate use of both traditional textures and natural materials allow the architecture to perfectly blend into the natural environment. The flat-tile roof, the metal eaves, the foundation that was made of Australian sandstone, and the slate walls are examples of the perfect combination of nature and technology, as well as oriental and Western aesthetics. The overall design of the Hotel strikes a balance between the feel of a formal ceremony and that of a leisure resort, imparting a sense of understated luxury and otherworldly elegance that is commensurate with the image of an open lakeside resort hotel.

| Materials samples of the public areas

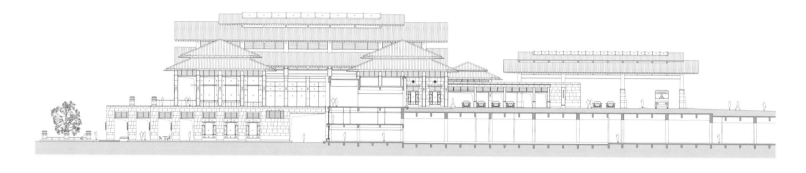

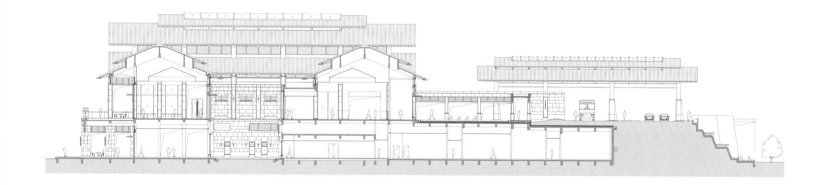

| Elevations of the lobby

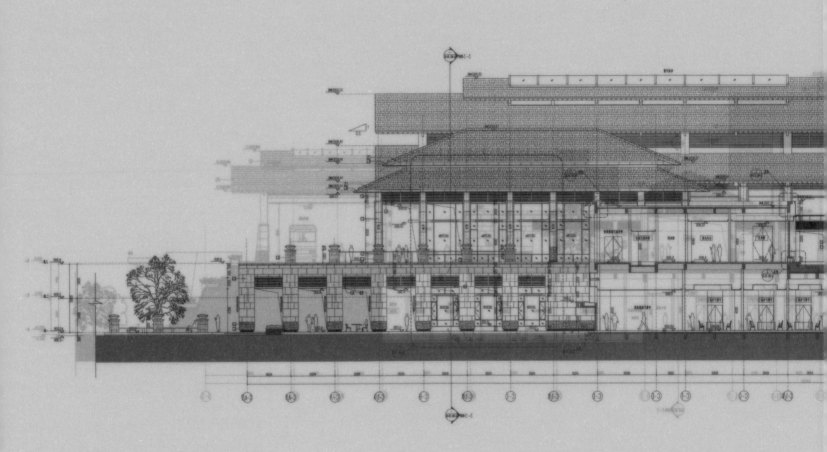

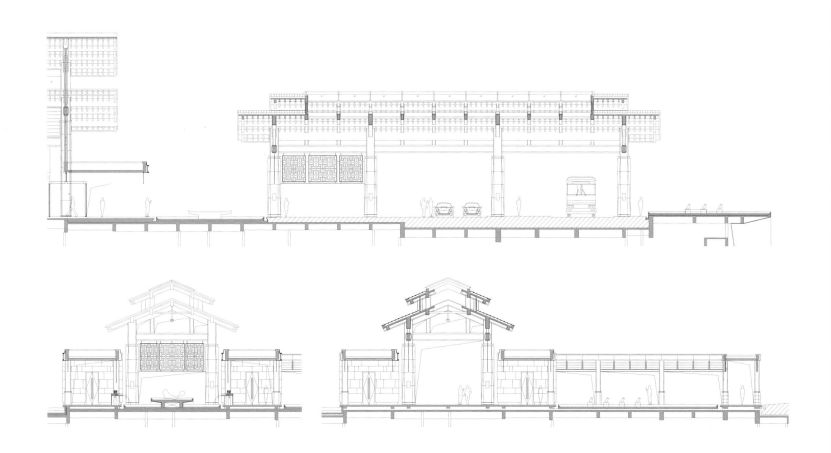

| Elevations of the front canopy

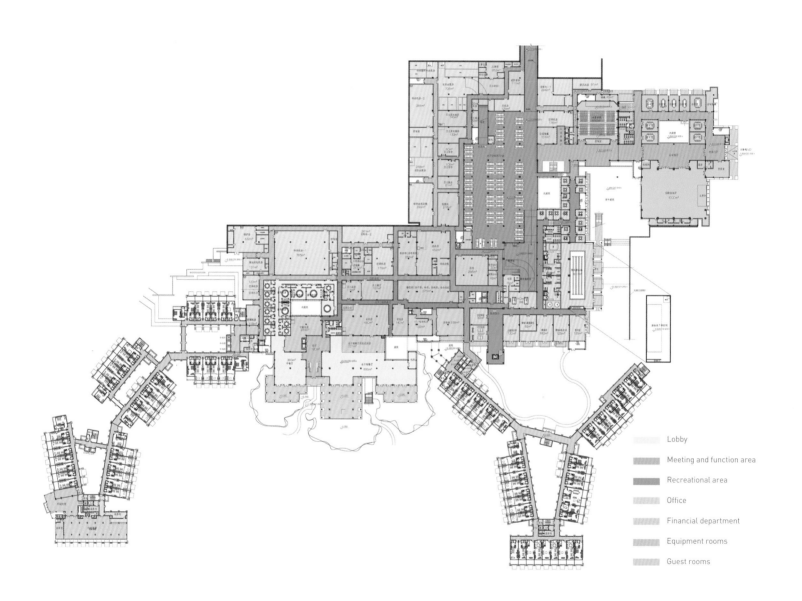

| Plan of the ground floor

Legend:
- Lobby
- Meeting and function area
- Recreational area
- Office
- Financial department
- Equipment rooms
- Guest rooms

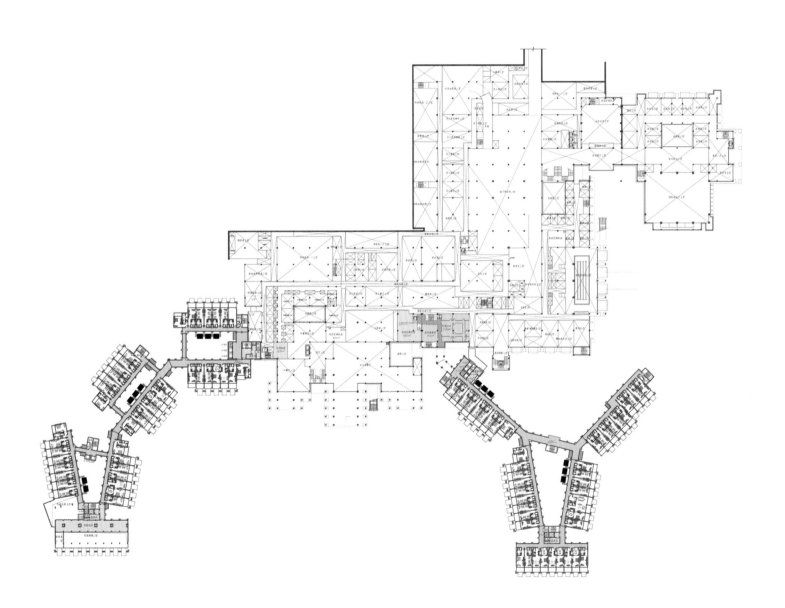

| Plan of the first floor

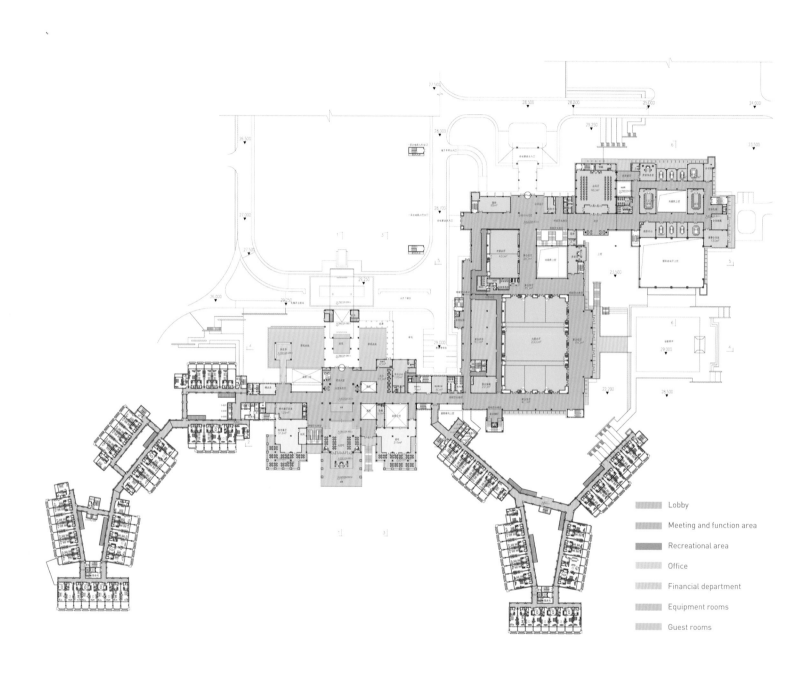

	Lobby
	Meeting and function area
	Recreational area
	Office
	Financial department
	Equipment rooms
	Guest rooms

| Plan of the second floor

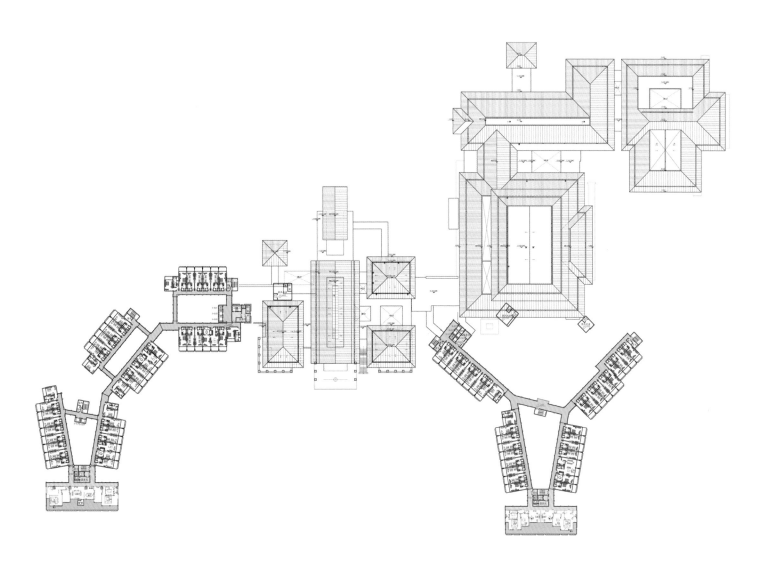

| Plan of the fifth floor

Construction

"God lives in details"

Construction

From design to construction, the design team spent a significant amount of time and effort on the critical elements of the details. In the process, the team applied for six design patents for fine details such as the metal eaves, the hidden drainage system, and the slate walls. The metal eaves, giving an industrial feel, add to the neat and solid image of the public lounge. These eaves are smooth, sharp, fine, and easy to install. The wooden planks and the sprung structures were designed to ensure the overall look is seamless. At the same time, both the coarse texture of the flat tiles and the natural lines on the wooden planks under the eaves introduce some natural elements to the design. Further, the drainage system is cleverly hidden in the joints to minimize the surface width of the draining pipes on the rooftop without compromising the capacity of the drainage system or the coherence of the roof's overall appearance. Moreover, natural original materials were used where possible to fit the ambience of the resort hotel. The grayish black slate, providing a sense of nature and resort feel, was widely used for all the walls in the guest areas.

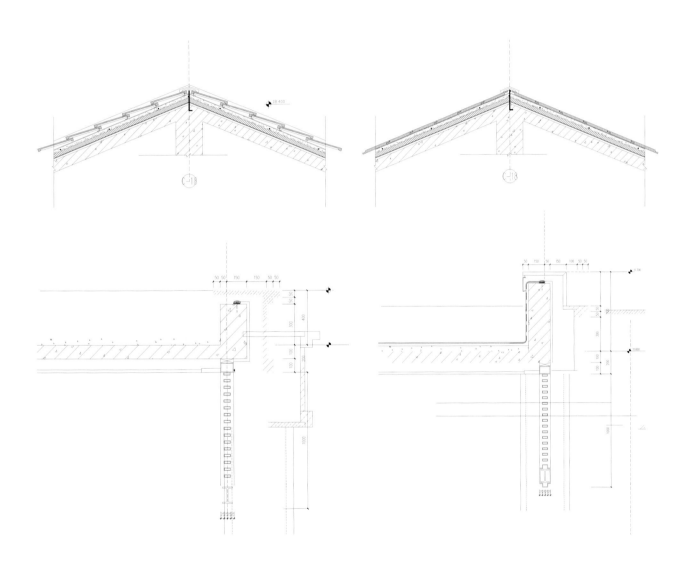

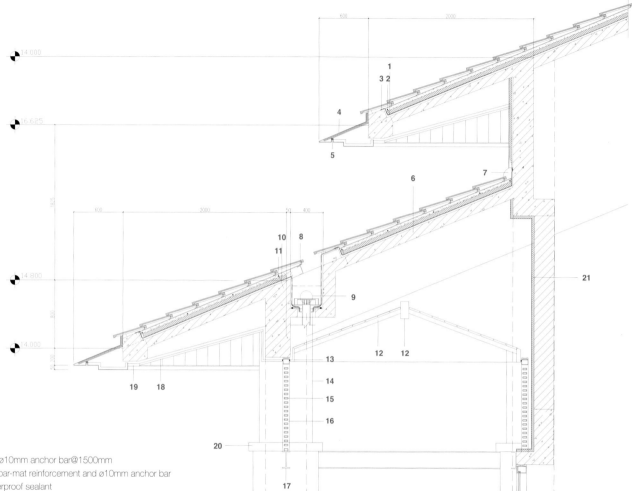

1 Embedded with ø10mm anchor bar@1500mm
2 Fixed by ø6mm bar-mat reinforcement and ø10mm anchor bar
3 Sealed with waterproof sealant
4 3mm monolayer aluminum plate with sound insulating layer and
  drainage system
5 Drip line
6 Specially made painted pottery roof tile
  Roof batten L30mm×4mm, with mid range as per tile
  specification
  Counter batten 25mm×4mm @600mm
  40mm C20 fine-stone concrete leveling layer with
  ø6mm@500mm×500mm bar-mat reinforcement
  50mm extruded polystyrene insulation board
  4mm polyester II high-polymer modified bituminous
  waterproof sheet
  1.5mm eco friendly polyurethane waterproofing paint
  20mm 1:2.5 cement-mortar leveling layer
  Reinforced-concrete roof board

7 Sealed by polymer cement mortar
8 10#zinc bath bounded with embedded beam components
9 Embedded with ø150mm stainless steel tube
10 Embedded with ø10mm anchor bar@1500mm
11 Fixed by ø6mm bar-mat reinforcement and ø10mm anchor bar
12 Decorative wood-like components
13 External plate
14 21mm exterior carbonized anti-corrosive plate cladding column
15 50mm×20mm wood-like aluminum alloy louver, sprayed with
  fluorocarbon
16 50mm×80mm wood-like aluminum alloy, sprayed with
  fluorocarbon

17 20b I-beam, tips-cut, sprayed with fluorocarbon
18 Light steel keel, 21mm×140mm exterior
  carbonized anti-corrosive wood notch plate ceiling
19 Trimmed with 30mm×140mm exterior carbonized
  anti-corrosive wood
20 Dry-hang stone
21 Advanced coating finish of the exterior wall behind
  louvers, waterproof flexible putty
  5mm polymer anti-crack mortar surface
  30mm extruded polystyrene foam sheet
  (insulated), bounded with special adhesives and
  fixed with anchors

The metal eaves add to the neat and solid images of the roof.

| Hidden drainage system on the rooftop

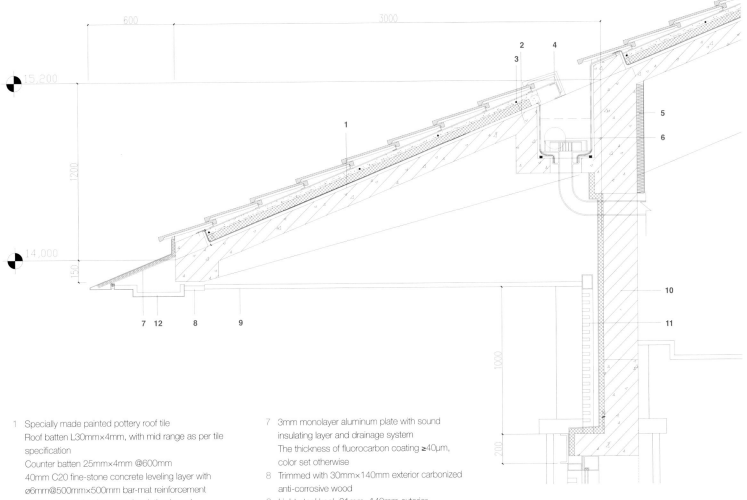

1 Specially made painted pottery roof tile
  Roof batten L30mm×4mm, with mid range as per tile specification
  Counter batten 25mm×4mm @600mm
  40mm C20 fine-stone concrete leveling layer with ø6mm@500mm×500mm bar-mat reinforcement
  50mm extruded polystyrene insulation board
  4mm polyester II high-polymer modified bituminous waterproof sheet
  1.5mm ecofriendly polyurethane waterproofing paint
  20mm 1:2.5 cement-mortar leveling layer
  Reinforced-concrete roof board
2 Embedded with ø10mm anchor bar@1500mm
3 Fixed by ø6mm bar-mat reinforcement and ø10mm anchor bar
4 10#zinc bath bounded with embedded beam components
5 Locally attached with 50mm rock wool plate, sealed with aluminum foil surface
6 Embedded with ø150mm stainless steel tube

7 3mm monolayer aluminum plate with sound insulating layer and drainage system
  The thickness of fluorocarbon coating ≥40μm, color set otherwise
8 Trimmed with 30mm×140mm exterior carbonized anti-corrosive wood
9 Light steel keel, 21mm×140mm exterior carbonized anti-corrosive wood notch plate ceiling
10 Advanced coating finish of the exterior wall behind louvers, waterproof flexible putty
  5mm polymer anti-crack mortar surface (containing two layers of alkali-resistant fiberglass mesh)
  30mm extruded polystyrene foam sheet (insulated), bounded with special adhesives and fixed with anchors
11 50mm×20mm wood-like aluminum alloy louver, sprayed with fluorocarbon
12 Drip line

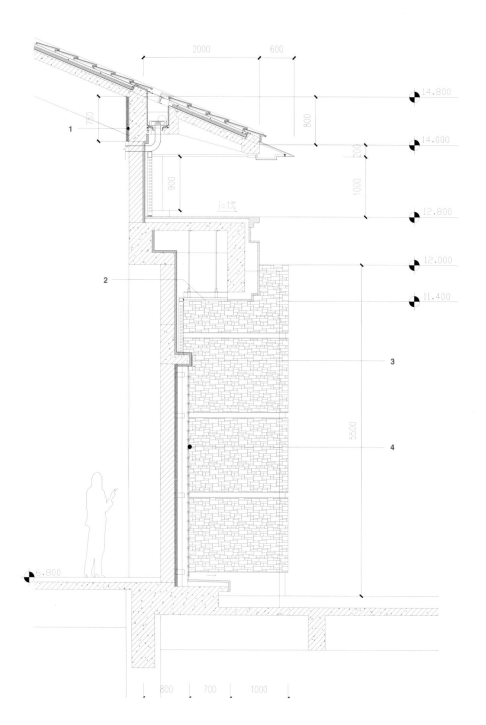

2000   600

14.800

800

14.000

900

1000

12.800

i=1%

12.000

11.400

1

2

3

5500

4

6.800

800   700   1000

1 Locally attached with 50mm rock wool plate, sealed with
   aluminum foil surface
2 Light steel keel, 21mm×140mm exterior carbonized anti-
   corrosive wood notch plate ceiling
3 Gray fluorocarbon coating steel profile
4 Wood-like stacked-plate wall surface

| Stacked-slate wall's surface

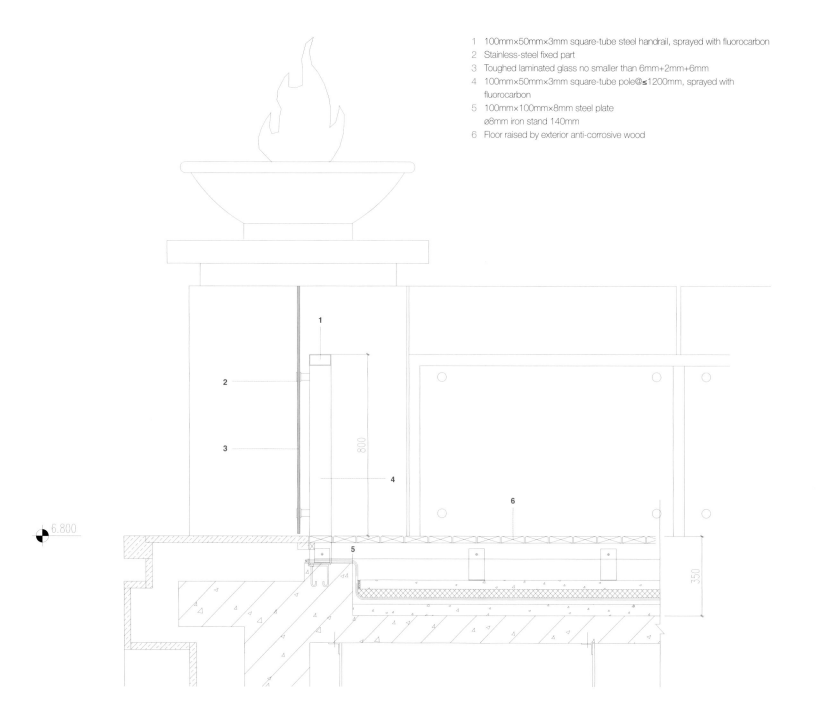

1 100mm×50mm×3mm square-tube steel handrail, sprayed with fluorocarbon
2 Stainless-steel fixed part
3 Toughed laminated glass no smaller than 6mm+2mm+6mm
4 100mm×50mm×3mm square-tube pole@≤1200mm, sprayed with fluorocarbon
5 100mm×100mm×8mm steel plate
  ø8mm iron stand 140mm
6 Floor raised by exterior anti-corrosive wood

| Glass fence with hidden handrail

| Lobby lounge

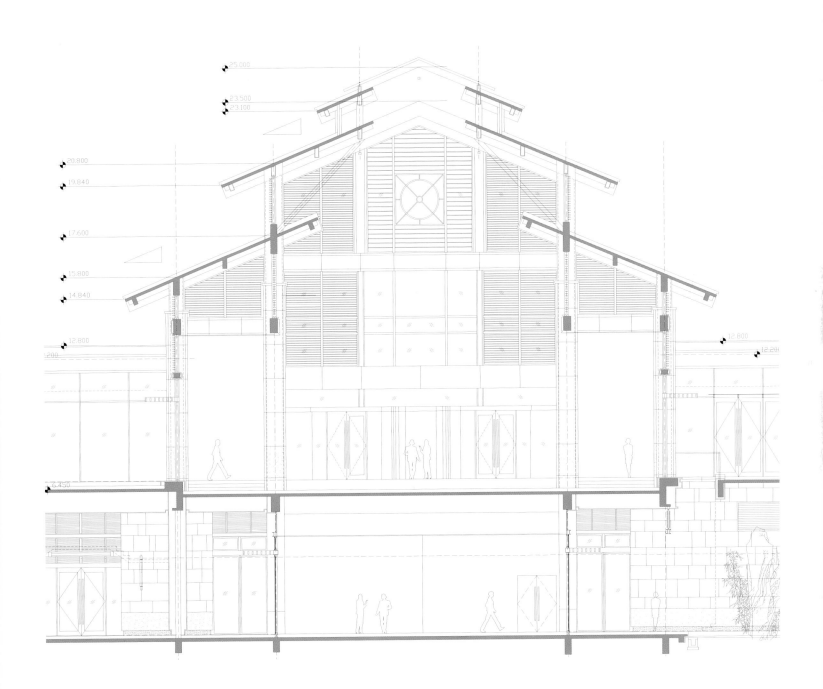

25.000

23.500
23.100

20.800

19.840

17.600

15.800

14.840

12.800   12.800
12.200   12.200

6.450

| Lobby lounge

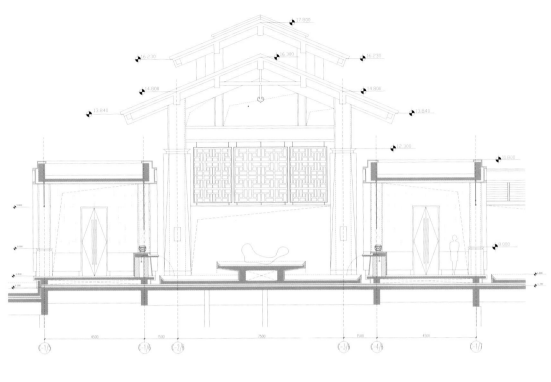

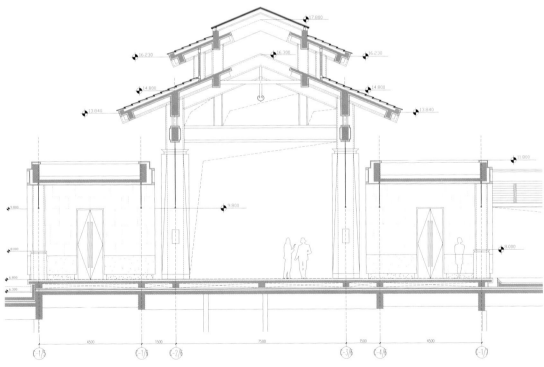

| Drop-off canopy

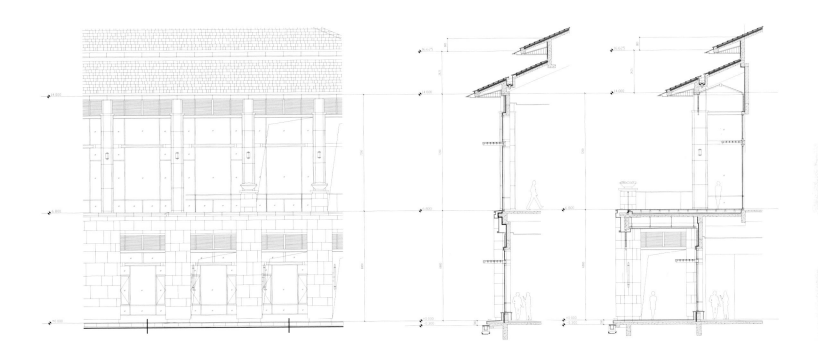

The bar, El Valle

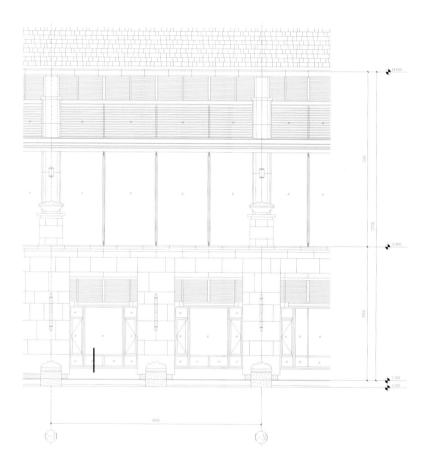
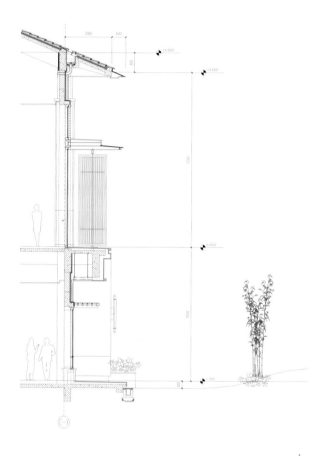

| Ballrooms

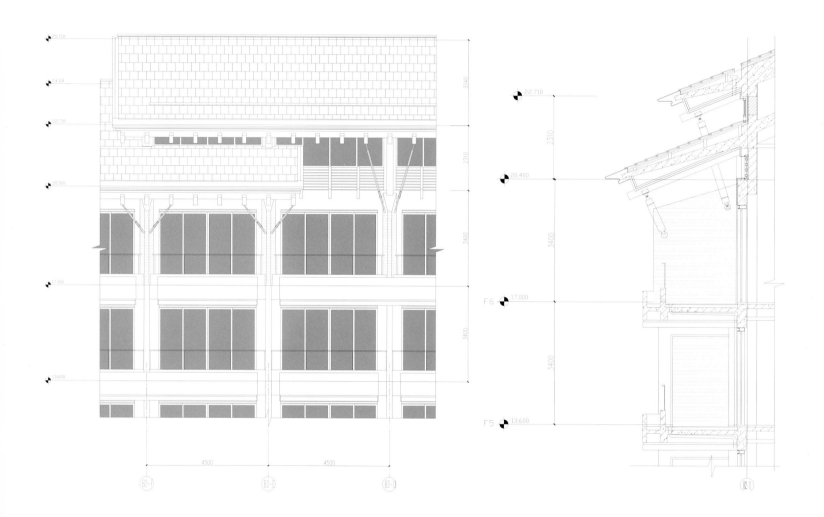

| Guest rooms

1   D20 drainage system, ∅3000mm
2   3mm monolayer aluminum plate with sound
    insulating layer and drainage system
    The thickness of fluorocarbon coating ≥30μm, color
    set otherwise
3   50mm exterior carbonized anti-corrosive gable board
4   Aluminum alloy wood-like components
5   Light steel keel, 21mm×140mm exterior carbonized
    anti-corrosive wood notch plate ceiling
6   Aluminum alloy window
    Coating surface (dark gray)
    Attached with 55mm aluminum foil fireproofing rock
    wool insulation board (Grade A)
7   Polymer cement mortar (with the same color to that
    of tiles)
8   Specially made painted pottery roof tile
    Roof batten L30mm×4mm, with mid range as per tile
    specification
    Angle-steel support
    1.5mm ecofriendly polyurethane waterproofing paint
    20mm 1:2.5 cement-mortar leveling layer
    Reinforced-concrete roof board

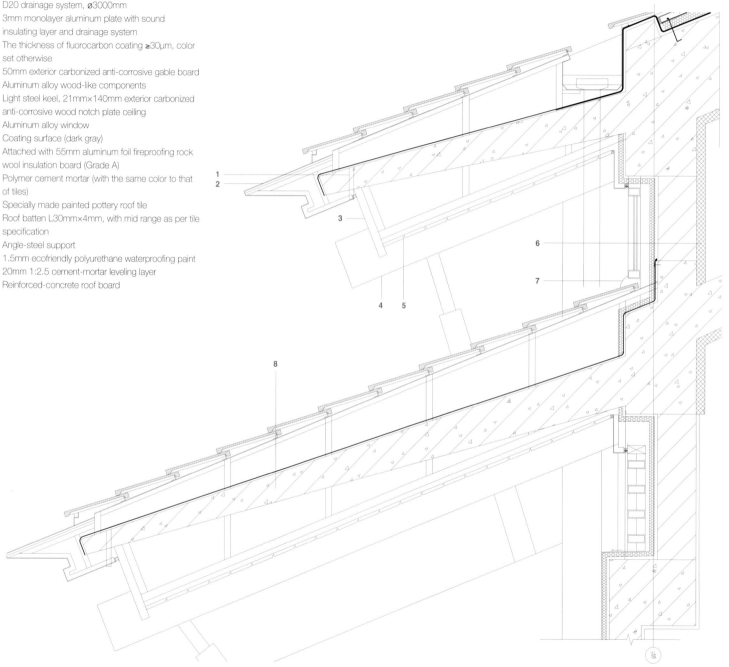

I Roof nodes

1 3mm monolayer aluminum plate with
  sound insulating layer and drainage
  system
  The thickness of fluorocarbon coating
  ≥40μm, color set otherwise
2 Light steel keel, 21mm×140mm exterior
  carbonized anti-corrosive wood notch
  plate ceiling
3 Trimmed with 30mm×140mm exterior
  carbonized anti-corrosive wood
4 Planting medium
  Geotextile filtering layer
  150mm pottery gravel/pebble drainage
  layer embedded with punched water pipe
  50mm C30 fine stone concrete
  (ø6mm@200mm double bi-directional bar-
  mat reinforcement)
  Polyethylene isolating layer
  4mm copper-composite-substrate
  modified-asphalt root-resistant membrane
  1.5mm ecofriendly polyurethane
  waterproofing paint (S type)
  20mm 1:2.5 cement-mortar leveling layer
  50mm extruded polystyrene insulation board
  1:8 pottery gravel concrete, the thinnest
  30mm, laid to falls of 1%
  Waterproof reinforced-concrete roof of the
  basement
5 Protected by 200mm non-clay sintered
  brick

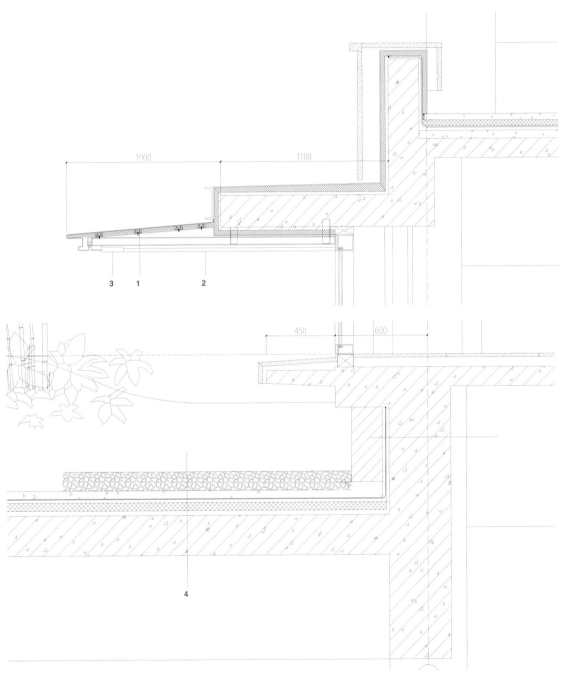

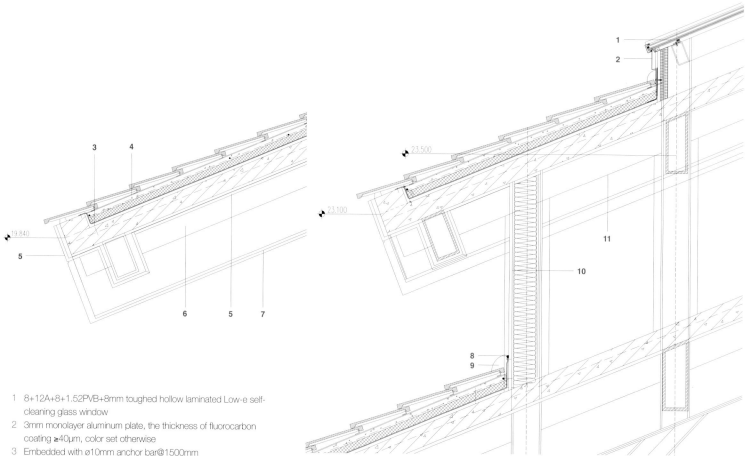

1 8+12A+8+1.52PVB+8mm toughed hollow laminated Low-e self-cleaning glass window
2 3mm monolayer aluminum plate, the thickness of fluorocarbon coating ≥40μm, color set otherwise
3 Embedded with ø10mm anchor bar@1500mm
   Fixed by ø6mm bar-mat reinforcement and ø10mm anchor bar
4 Specially made painted pottery roof tile
   Roof batten L30mm×4mm, with mid range as per tile specification
   Counter batten 25mm×4mm @600mm
   400mm C20 fine-stone concrete leveling layer with
   ø6mm@500mm×500mm bar-mat reinforcement
   50mm extruded polystyrene insulation board
   4mm polyester II high-polymer modified bituminous waterproof sheet
   1.5mm ecofriendly polyurethane waterproofing paint
   20mm 1:2.5 cement-mortar leveling layer
   Reinforced-concrete roof board
5 21mm exterior carbonized anti-corrosive plate cladding
6 100mm×150mm wood-like aluminum profile
7 21mm exterior carbonized anti-corrosive plate
8 Waterproofing sealant

9 Sealed with polymer cement mortar
10 Advanced exterior paint
   Painted with 20mm steel wire mesh and cement mortar
   12mm fiber-reinforced calcium-silicate-board wall panels
   A layer of waterproofing breathable membrane
   Light steel keel
   150mm rock wool insulated sound-proofing layer
   PVC air-insulation layer
   12mm×2mm plaster slab
   Interior latex paint
11 Steel roof truss
   Painted with thin-layered fire-retardant coating, fireproof limit of 1.5 hours, overcoating set otherwise

I Roof nodes

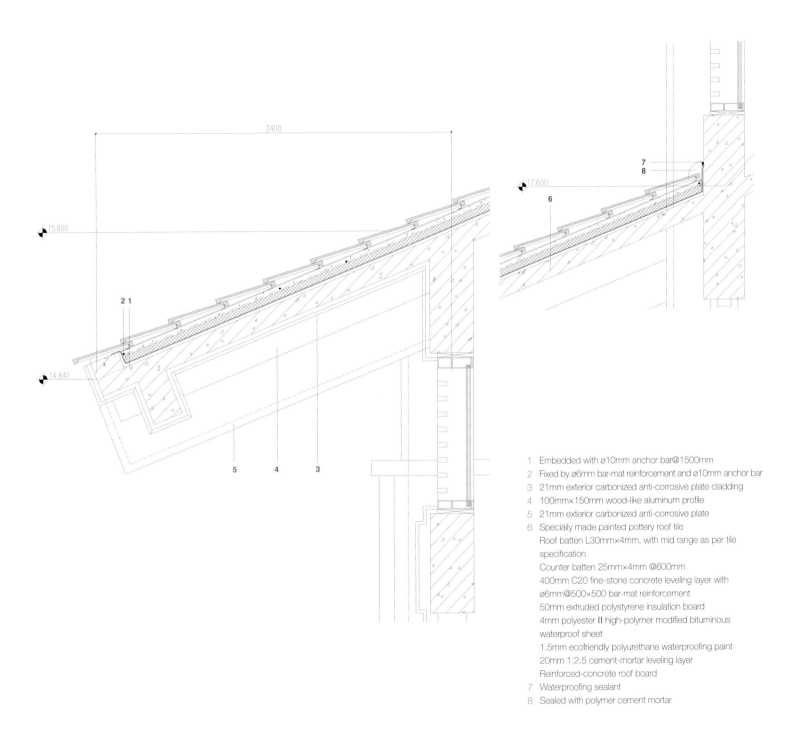

1 Embedded with ø10mm anchor bar@1500mm
2 Fixed by ø6mm bar-mat reinforcement and ø10mm anchor bar
3 21mm exterior carbonized anti-corrosive plate cladding
4 100mm×150mm wood-like aluminum profile
5 21mm exterior carbonized anti-corrosive plate
6 Specially made painted pottery roof tile
   Roof batten L30mm×4mm, with mid range as per tile
   specification
   Counter batten 25mm×4mm @600mm
   400mm C20 fine-stone concrete leveling layer with
   ø6mm@500×500 bar-mat reinforcement
   50mm extruded polystyrene insulation board
   4mm polyester II high-polymer modified bituminous
   waterproof sheet
   1.5mm ecofriendly polyurethane waterproofing paint
   20mm 1:2.5 cement-mortar leveling layer
   Reinforced-concrete roof board
7 Waterproofing sealant
8 Sealed with polymer cement mortar

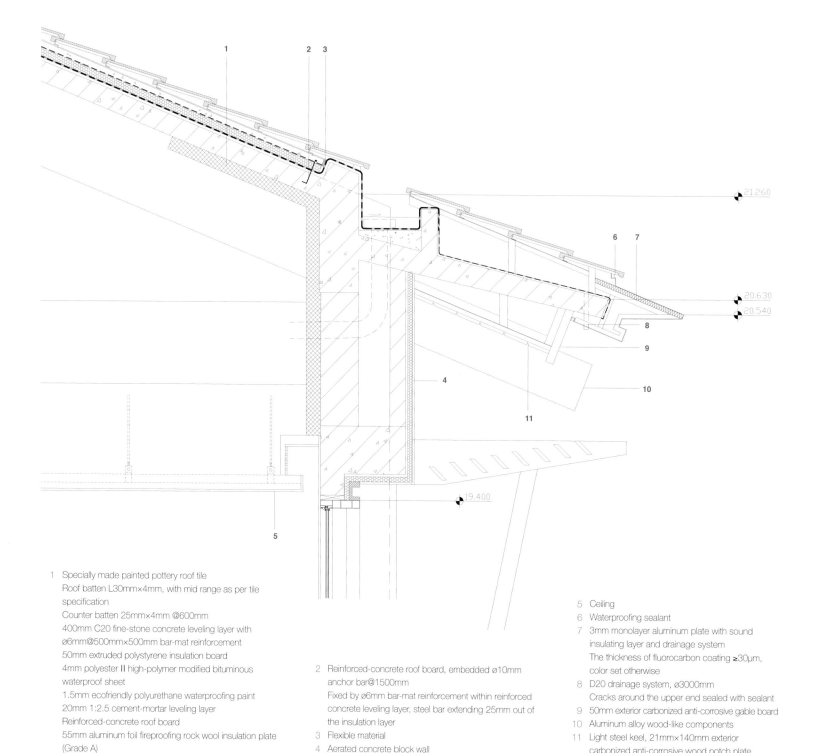

1 Specially made painted pottery roof tile
  Roof batten L30mm×4mm, with mid range as per tile specification
  Counter batten 25mm×4mm @600mm
  400mm C20 fine-stone concrete leveling layer with ø6mm@500mm×500mm bar-mat reinforcement
  50mm extruded polystyrene insulation board
  4mm polyester II high-polymer modified bituminous waterproof sheet
  1.5mm ecofriendly polyurethane waterproofing paint
  20mm 1:2.5 cement-mortar leveling layer
  Reinforced-concrete roof board
  55mm aluminum foil fireproofing rock wool insulation plate (Grade A)

2 Reinforced-concrete roof board, embedded ø10mm anchor bar@1500mm
  Fixed by ø6mm bar-mat reinforcement within reinforced concrete leveling layer, steel bar extending 25mm out of the insulation layer

3 Flexible material

4 Aerated concrete block wall

5 Ceiling

6 Waterproofing sealant

7 3mm monolayer aluminum plate with sound insulating layer and drainage system
  The thickness of fluorocarbon coating ≥30μm, color set otherwise

8 D20 drainage system, ø3000mm
  Cracks around the upper end sealed with sealant

9 50mm exterior carbonized anti-corrosive gable board

10 Aluminum alloy wood-like components

11 Light steel keel, 21mm×140mm exterior carbonized anti-corrosive wood notch plate

I Roof nodes

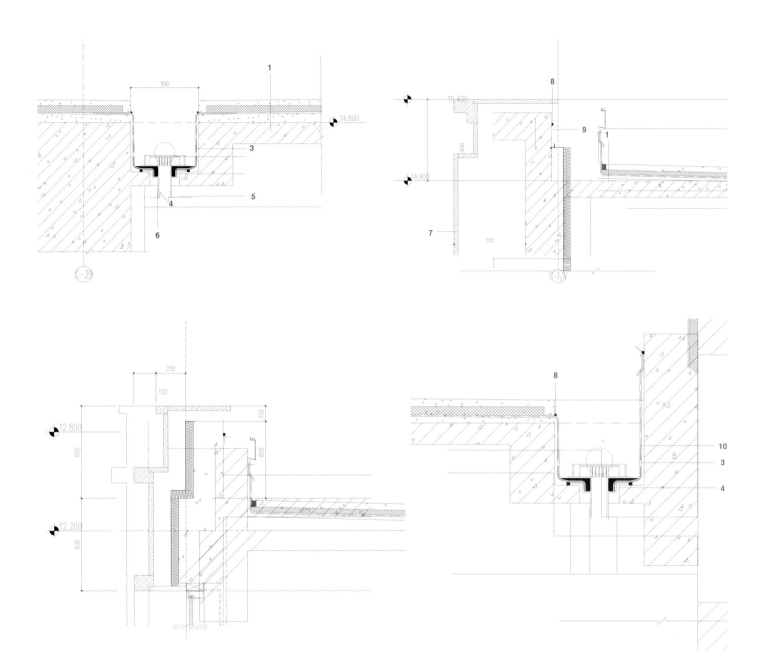

1 Flat roof
2 Embedded with ø150mm stainless-steel tube
3 Two layers of reinforced materials is coated at the
   waterproofing layer of the outfall, totally 3mm
4 Model 87 roof drain
5 Filled with C15 fine-stone concrete
6 Sealed with waterproofing sealant

7 30mm dry-hang granite curtain wall
8 Waterproofing sealant
9 1.5mm aluminum flashing sheet
10 Gutter waterproofing layer and additional
   waterproofing layer

| Construction site

Hilton Wuhan Optics Valley

| Construction site

Realization

"A gift to the city"

| Drop-off

| Pavilions and water feature

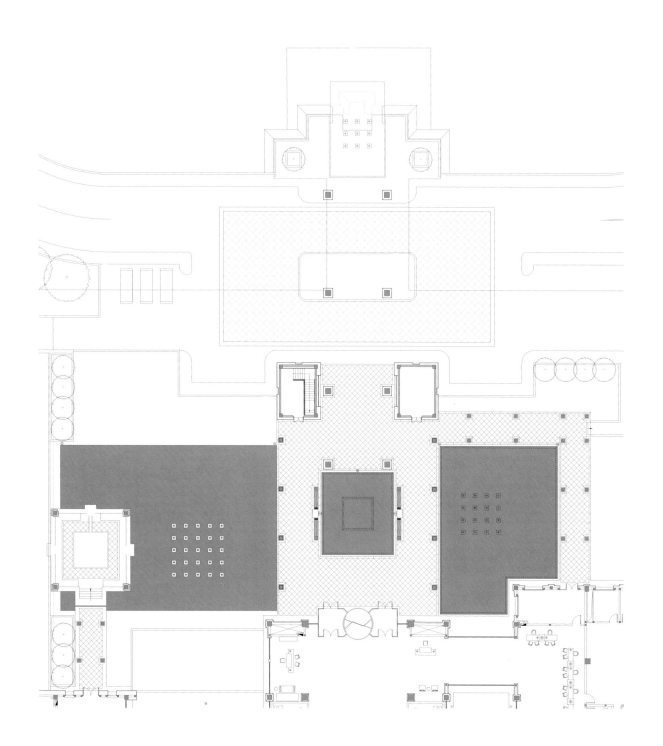

| Front canopy

| Lobby lounge

| Front desk and lobby lounge

Opposite	Magnificent exterior of the lobby
Left	View from lobby to central garden
Right	View from central garden to lobby

| Exterior of the lobby lounge 1

| Exterior of the lobby lounge 2

| Bar "El Valle"

All-day dining at Chinachops

Top	Semi-outdoor dining area
Bottom	Interior of the dining room
Opposite	Interior of the private dining room

Cucina, the Italian restaurant

| Yuxi, the Chinese restaurant

Hilton Wuhan Optics Valley

| Yuxi, the Chinese restaurant

CENTRAL GARDEN

| Panorama of the central garden

Hilton Wuhan Optics Valley

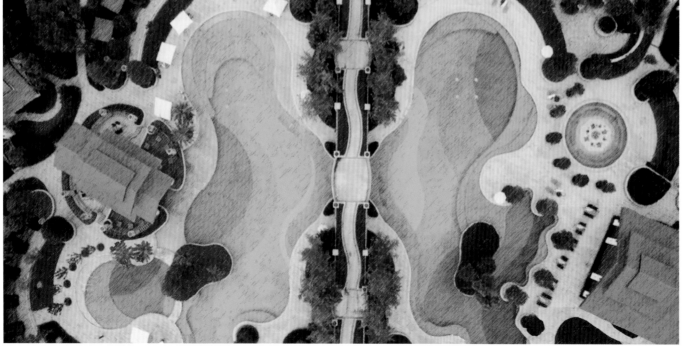

| Swimming pool

1　300mm×500mm×47mm yellow rustic granite litchi
　　finish cap
2　Drainage
3　200mm×150mm×25mm yello rustic granite litchi finish
　　"seamless"
4　200mm reinforced concrete
　　100mm concrete
　　100mm gravel
　　95% compacted soil
5　600mm×450mm×50mm yellow rustic granite litchi
　　finish "seamless"
　　20mm cement mortar
　　Cement-based waterproof coating
　　20mm cement mortar leveling
6　20mm×20mm×20mm glass mosaic

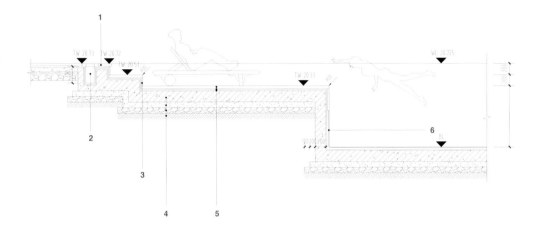

1　Wood-color aluminum-alloy decorative louvers
2　300mm×300mm×50mm yellow rustic granite,
　　litchi finish
3　Pool and spa equipment area
4　M7.5mm cement mortar masonry MU10mm standard brick
　　100mm concrete
　　100mm gravel
　　90% compacted soil
5　25mm×25mm×5mm blue glass mosaic (polished finish)
　　20mm 1:2.5 cement mortar
　　3mm SBS waterproofing
　　20mm 1:2.5 cement-mortar leveling layer
6　20mm C25 reinforced concrete (ø10mm @150mm
　　double layer rebar)
　　100mm C15 concrete
　　100mm gravel
　　90% compacted soil
7　25mm×25mm×25mm blue glass mosaic
　　M7.5mm cement mortar masonry
　　MU10mm standard brick

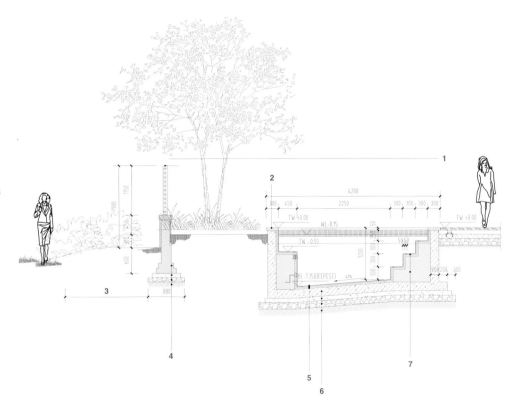

|　Nodes of the swimming pool

| Waterfront terrace

1　1300mm×2000mm×24mm double-layer
　　laminated tempered glass
2　200mm×200mm×5mm matte aluminum box
　　Anchored with deck by chemically bounded rebar
3　L×150mm×40mm merbau antiseptic timber
4　600mm module
5　T-shape clip
6　50mm×30mm joist
7　50mm×30mm×3mm galvanized steel@400mm
　　Anchored by M8mm expansion bolts
8　Double-layer laminated tempered glass
9　50mm×5mm U-shape anchor (welding with steel
　　plate)
　　Silicone rubber seal
10　200mm×200mm×5mm embedded steel plate
　　Chemically bounded rebar
11　L×150mm×50mm antiseptic timber
12　50mm×50mm antiseptic joist
　　150mm reinforced concrete

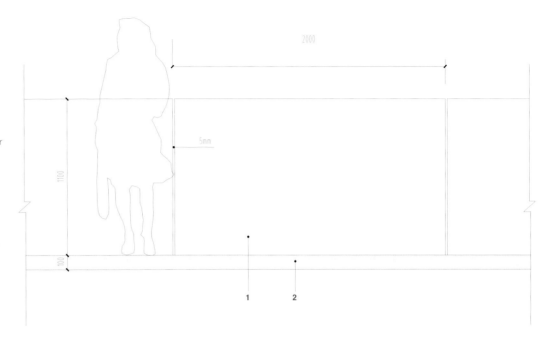

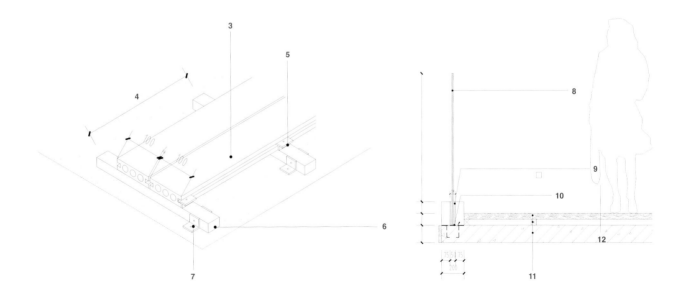

| Nodes of the waterfront terrace

Opposite | Exterior of the ballrooms
Top | Entrance of the international convention center

Opposite | Water feature of central garden
Top | Exterior of the convention center

Hilton Wuhan Optics Valley

| Sunken cascade courtyard

The Magpie Bridge connecting ballrooms with the wedding lawn

Top | Cascade walls
Bottom | Sunken courtyard and the Magpie Bridge

| The Magpie Bridge

| Sunken cascade courtyard

Hilton Wuhan Optics Valley

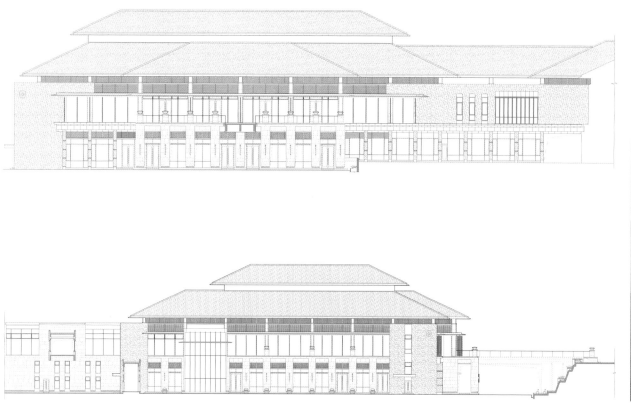

| Internal courtyard of the convention center

Hilton Wuhan Optics Valley

| Internal courtyard of the convention center

Hilton Wuhan Optics Valley

| Corridors of the ballrooms

Top | Small ballrooms
Opposite top | Banquet scene of grand ballrooms
Opposite bottom | Meeting scene of grand ballrooms

Top left | Presence chamber
Top right | Hall of the convention center
Bottom | Boardroom

| Auditorium

Realization

| Indoor swimming pool

健身中心
FITNESS CENTER

Opposite	Fitness center and rest area
Top	Sauna room
Bottom	Fitness center

| Guest rooms

| Exquisite elevation details

| Deluxe room with pool and lake view

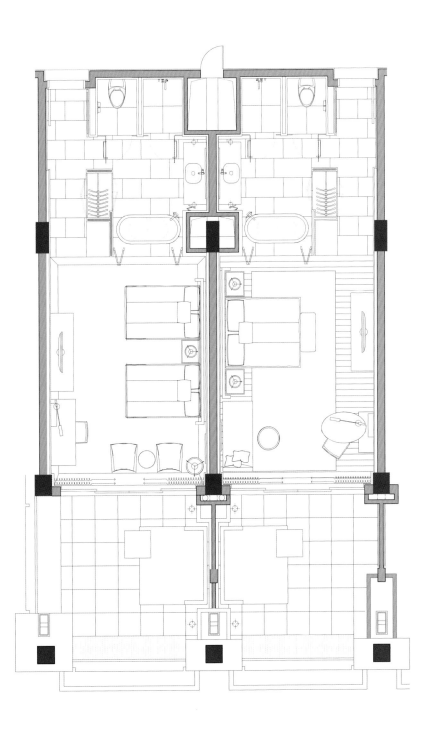

Hilton Wuhan Optics Valley

| King one-bedroom suite with two balconies

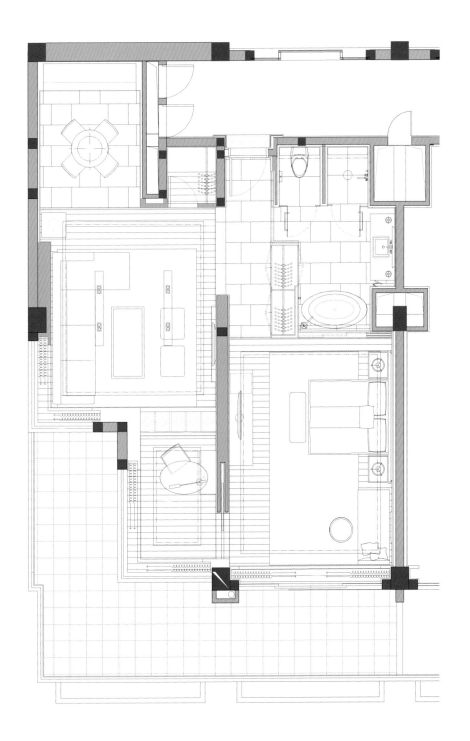

Hilton Wuhan Optics Valley

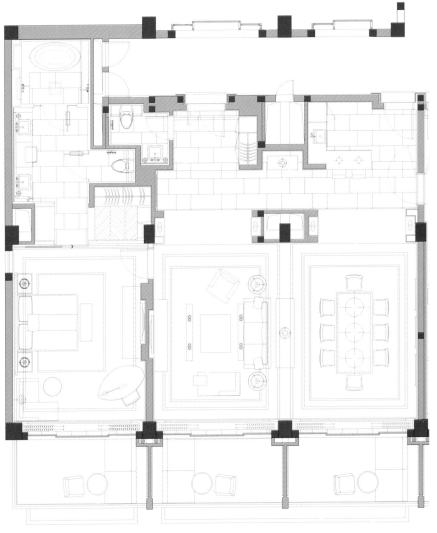

| King one-bedroom suite with three balconies

| Executive lounge

Hilton Wuhan Optics Valley

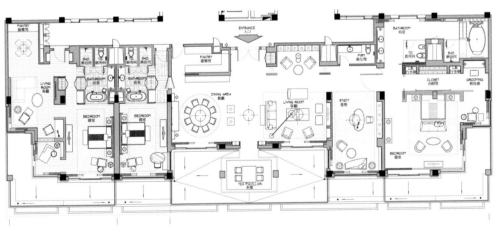

| King presidential suite

| King presidential suite

Hilton Wuhan Optics Valley

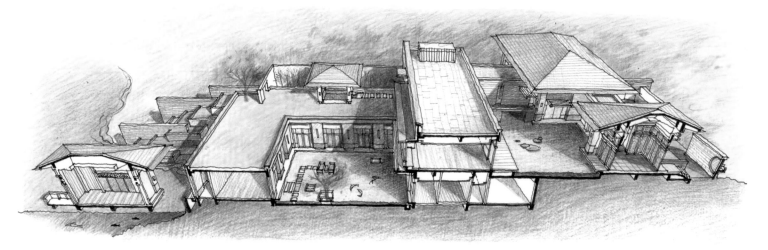

| Spa area

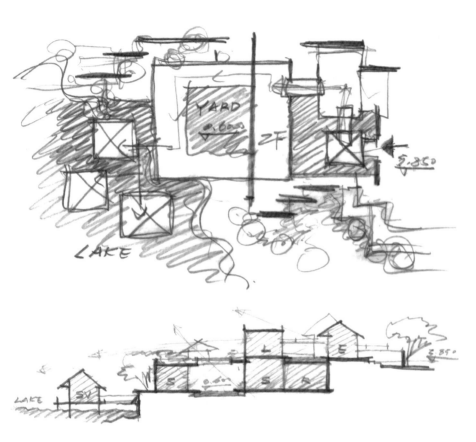

| Sections of the spa area

Hilton Wuhan Optics Valley

High-quality results

results

"The great shokunin"

High-quality results

A comparison between the blueprint and the actual completed hotel shows a close match. The high quality of construction and finishing is firstly attributable to a well thought out design that perfectly matched the demands of the hotel management company and the owners. The designers insisted on a "re-design" strategy during the design of construction drawings. Construction drawings are not simply a charting work, but a process of continuously refining the details and controlling the quality of the key elements.

Fortunately, the team did not go through any major change in the overall design during the whole process from master plan to construction drawings, and was able to focus on fine-tuning of the original design that was pinned down during the bidding. The Project has altogether more than 1000 construction drawings, all verified by 3D models. During the design and construction process, numerous enlarged façade drawings, cross-sectional drawings, and joint specification drawings were used to achieve the final finish.

Turning such a fine design from drawings to reality owes to the collective effort by the owners, the designers, and the constructors. The end product is well designed and well constructed; the hard work of the entire project team has turned the Hotel into Huashan New Town's crown jewel, and a critical milestone in Central China's development.

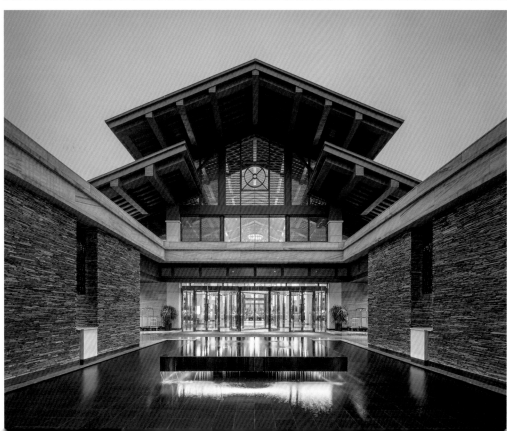

Hilton Wuhan Optics Valley

Hilton Wuhan Optics Valley

Credits

The story of a landmark resort
2009-2017

"Pearls in central China"

Competition
Wuhan SEP 2009

"Beauty is forever"

Design Development
Shanghai APR 2010

Schematic Design
Shanghai NOV 2009

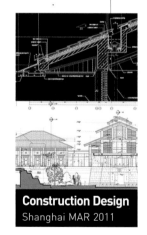

Construction Design
Shanghai MAR 2011

"God lives in details"

"A pastoral symphony of paradise"

2009　　　　2010　　　　2011

"Dreams come true"

Construction Starts
Wuhan MAY 2011

"A gift to the city"

Opening Ceremony
Wuhan DEC 2013

Publishing Finishes
Shanghai DEC 2016

2012 • 2013 • 2014 • 2015 • 2016 • 2017

Construction
Wuhan FEB 2012

"The great shokunin"

Publishing Starts
Shanghai APR 2016

**"Process is tortuous,
results are good."**

PROJECT DATA

Name	Hilton Wuhan Optics Valley
Owner	Wuhan Eco City Country Garden Investment, Ltd.
Location	No. 9 Chunhe Road, Huashan Eco City East Lake High Tech Dev Zone, Wuhan, China
Building Area	117,000 square meters
Building Height	23.6 meters
Date of Competition	September 2009
Date of Design	October 2009 – March 2011
Date of Opening	December 2013

LIU Xingnian

President of Hubei United Investment Group
Chief Commander of Wuhan Huashan Eco City

OWNER

Wuhan Eco City Country Garden Investment, Ltd.

(founded by Hubei United Investment Group & Country Garden Group)

Chairman	DUAN Yu
Chairman	YU Zhongquan
President	CHEN Xuanke
Vice President	YU Minghua
Vice President	SHEN Xin
Chief Financial Officer	QI Gui
General Manager of Hotel Project	CHEN Tao
Vice President	YE Wei
Design Director of Hotel Project	ZHANG Fan
Civil Engineering	CAO Bingwen
Senior Engineer of Interior Decoration	WANG Jianping
Senior Engineer of Facade Decoration	FANG Yi
Senior Electrical and Mechanical Engineer	ZHAO Wen

LING Kege Project Chief

LING Kege is the chief architect of Dushe Design Shanghai. He holds
a Bachelor of Architecture from Chongqing University. He has over
15 years of experience in the field of architecture design. He is the
project chief of Hilton Wuhan Optics Valley.

DESIGN ARCHITECT

Chief Creator Architect	XU Qi
Architect Director	WANG Limin, CHEN Yu
Design Team	LIU Yijia, CHEN Tianduo, JIANG Meng, LIU Wenjun, HU Wei, ZHANG Zhenlian
Interior Design of Lobby	LING Kege, XU Qi

INTERIOR DESIGN
Hirsch Bedner Associates, USA

Partner	Fiona BAGAMAN
Senior Designer	Karoline RAKOWSKA
Project Designer	Constantino GARCIA
Designers	Eva CHAN, Joel WAN

LANDSCAPE DESIGN
Peridian International Inc., USA

Principal	Rae L. PRICE, FASLA

TOPOS Landscape Architects, USA

Principal	ZHU Yi, RLA California
Design Team	WANG Xiaoquan, FANG Minghua, Rob PARKER, WANG Guangyan, JIAO Wenjia

LIGHTING DESIGN
Relux & Relux Lighting Design Consultant, China

STRUCTURAL ENGINEER
East China Architectural Design & Research Institute, China

Project Manager	ZHOU Wei
Design Team	SHI Zhishen, RU Lin, ZHANG Feng, LING Bingchuan

HVAC, PLUMBING, ELECTRICAL, POWER, AND ECOLOGY ENGINEER
Beca Engineering Consulting (Shanghai), China
East China Architectural Design & Research Institute, China

Project Manager	CAO Chengshu
HVAC Director	LIU Lan
Plumbing Director	TAO Jun
Electrical Director	XU Xun
Power Director	DI Lingling
Ecology Director	YI Jianguang

AWARDS

Best Conference and Exhibition Hotel of the Year
Golden Horse Award of China Hotel, 2015—2016

Certificate of Excellence of the Year
TripAdvisor, 2016

Certificate of Excellence of the Year
TripAdvisor, 2015

Best New Luxury Hotel of the Year (Secondary/Third City)
China Travel & Meeting Industry Awards, 2014

PUBLICATIONS

LING Kege, XU Qi. "Space, Experience, Design: The Design of Wuhan Optics Valley Hilton,
Hubei [J]." *Time+Architecture*, 2014, (2)
LING Kege, XU Qi. "Hilton Wuhan Optics Valley [J]."
Urbanism and Architecture, 2015, (7)
JIANG Haina. "Taste is the Most Important Thing in Resort Hotel's Design: The Interview
about Hilton Optical Valley Resort & Spa in Wuhan [J]". *Architecture Technique*, 2011, (Z4)

BOOK TEAM IN SHANGHAI

Chief Editor — **XU Qi**

XU Qi is the partner of Dushe Design Shanghai. He holds a Master of Architecture from Southeast University and has been engaged in architecture design for 10 years. As the chief creator architect of Hilton Wuhan Optics Valley, he took charge of the coordination of materials and data organization of the book as a whole.

Team — CHENG Wen, GUO Sicong, QIU Peixin

Sketch drawings — XU Qi

IMAGES PUBLISHING EDITORIAL TEAM

CEO — **Paul LATHAM**

Paul LATHAM is the CEO of The Images Publishing Group and ACC Publishing & Distribution. Images Publishing is the world leader among architecture and design publishing houses, with worldwide distribution.

Production Manager — **Rod GILBERT**

Senior Editor — **Gina TSAROUHAS**

TRANSLATOR

GAO Yubing

PHOTOGRAPHERS

ZHANG Yong, ZYStudio, Shanghai

SU Shengliang, Shanghai